Behind the Wheel

The Great Automobile Aficionados

Translated from the French by Alan McKay
Design: Caroline Renouf
Copyediting: Penny Isaac
Typesetting: Claude-Olivier Four
Proofreading: Helen Downey
Color Separation: Reproscan, Bergamo
Printed in China by Toppan Leefung

Distributed in North America
by Rizzoli International Publications, Inc.

Simultaneously published
in French as *Les fous du volant*
© Flammarion, Paris, 2010

editions.flammarion.com

10 11 12   3 2 1

ISBN: 978-2-08-030154-3

Dépôt légal: 10/2010

Robert Puyal

Behind the Wheel
The Great Automobile Aficionados

Flammarion

Contents

The Turn of the Century

The Centaur's Path

For roads, they had horse tracks—clumsily paved, if paved at all. For cars, they had sorts of carriages, without shafts or horses. Did they have headlights, brakes? Hardly any. No windshield, barely any tires. But they did have blazing engines, vibrant and capricious, getting more powerful by the day. The chassis were heavy, like roof frames; the wheels had to be turned with both hands, sometimes with three: a mechanic had to be taken aboard. But there were men and women to goad on these mechanical monsters, up to speeds that, a century or so later, our dull carriages are not allowed to reach. These centaurs waged war against speed, threw themselves into races with planes, trains, and cars. There were long, deadly races; ones that nonetheless fascinated record crowds of pedestrians, cyclists, and riders. To think we don't even wear hats any more. We must have taken them off, as a tribute to their courage, their visionary stubbornness, and also to their beauty.

Camille Jenatzy
Camille du Gast
Louis Renault
Jules Bonnot
Jules Gout
Henry Ford

Camille Jenatzy

1868-1913

The Devil on a Mission

Imagine a little French road at Achères, between Poissy and Conflans-Sainte-Honorine, about 15 miles from Paris—a good hour and a half in a horse-drawn carriage.

A few officials were standing around with a whole assortment of precision timepieces. They wore mustaches and bowler hats, as usual: this was 1899.

They were gathered around a foreigner wearing a naval officer's uniform, including hat, and sporting a beautiful red beard. Among these officials were the representatives from the weekly, *France Automobile*. In December the previous year, the paper had put forward the idea of a simple speed race, and the big bearded man, a Belgian of Polish origin, was there to try and win it. He was Camille Jenatzy, but the newspapers quickly dubbed him the "Red Devil."

Beside him was his mount: a torpedo-shaped fuselage perched on a stool fitted with wheels. Above this, a hollow where he, Jenatzy, would have to position himself; underneath the "torpedo" was all that really mattered: two electric motors and wheels fitted with tires. His father, a rubber industrialist in Belgium, had made Jenatzy tires for bicycles as well as all sorts of other rubber items. But Camille had fitted his machine with the new Michelin tires, with extensible collars, which seemed to offer better protection against the dangers of punctures. This time it was the method of propulsion that was being promoted, with a view to getting a piece of the Parisian

electric hackney cab market. But sacrifices had to be made.

At the very end of the nineteenth century a car's normal speed was 10–25 mph (15–40 km/h). What was the point of going faster? Replacing the horse and its droppings was good enough. The idea of trying to outdo the horse's range, reliability, and speed—nobody was seriously thinking about anything like that. This was not very far from the medical debate as to whether human life could stand going beyond the natural speed of movement, in other words the roughly 30 mph (50 km/h) of a man riding a horse. This had been apropos of trains but, ever since, wagonloads of happy travelers had been proving the absurdity of what medical experts put about sometimes . . . apart from the dangers from bits of grit, of course. But trying to go fast aboard a car was another ball game altogether!

Jenatzy had had Léon Auscher build the coachwork; it recalled the shell-shaped vehicles you see on the engravings in Jules Verne's books. Three years later, on the same model, Méliès drew the lunar rocket that featured in his 1902 film, *Le Voyage dans la lune* (*Voyage to the Moon*). On Jenatzy's blue-gray shell, there was a banderole painted with the machine's name "*Jamais Contente*"—"Never Satisfied." Impertinence

Marcel Renault and Vauthier, his mechanic, slowed down after the control at Tours, during the 1903 Paris—Madrid race (p. 10). Shortly after Poitiers, Marcel was killed.

The Red Devil (facing page). Camille Jenatzy was a redhead, who raced like a devil in his wheezing, smoking car; he succeeded in reaching a speed of 41.66 mph, which soon became 65.62 mph.

is never very far beneath the surface when men are playing, and among these bowler-hatted men it was of course rumored that this was also Mme Jenatzy's sobriquet.

The comte de Chasseloup-Laubat, a respected sportsman, had been there three months earlier and fixed the first speed record at 40 mph (64 km/h), with an electric Jeantaud. Jeantaud was the other maker of electric cabs and the first of Jenatzy's rivals.

Quickly informed about this, Jenatzy turned up at once and reached a speed that went some way to explaining his nickname, 41 mph (66.6 km/h, or 666, the devil's number.) But Chasseloup took to the track again ten days later and took the record further, up to more than 50 mph (80 km/h).

An outlandish idea, once shared, quickly becomes a sort of sporting discipline. Jenatzy understood that outdoing the opposition wasn't enough, but how could he settle things? People were beginning to understand that speed was in fact an infinite dimension. To silence your adversaries, you had to break a good record, one for the history books.

Jenatzy set off. From a standing start his machine reached the first kilometer after 47 seconds, an average of 47.5 mph (76 km/h), without a windshield, and almost without brakes. There was no steering wheel, either: steering was very rudimentary, using a notched handlebar, rather like the rudder of a ship but much less effective. If the car started to veer off to one side or other of the road, it certainly wouldn't react promptly or effectively.

Amid the whirring of the two electric motors, *Jamais Contente* returned to the timing point, this time at full speed. Jenatzy, who had only been able to squeeze his legs inside the shell, was bent over the handlebars. You could make out his eyes wrinkled by the speed and you could feel the slipstream of the machine. Thirty-four seconds later, he was a thousand yards away, his beard blowing in the wind. The officials immediately calculated his speed: 66.176 mph, or 105.882 km/h. The famed 100 km/h. (62.5 mph) barrier had been passed and Jenatzy had broken through into world news with a roar. After this success and one or two others (in May of the same year, he officially reached more than 75 mph/120 km/h), Jenatzy was considered a great driver.

Boldness was a prerequisite for being "one of them," for being part of this élite, who were both acclaimed and derided. Half of them were mechanics or technicians like Jenatzy, and half of them aristocrats, which made for a motley collection of personalities, modern to the point of fanaticism yet with both chivalric and guardroom manners.

No doubt Jenatzy reached this point in his career willingly and remained there for commercial reasons. Finally he became an authority; his reputation meant that he was asked by the firm Mors to take part in an automobile Tour de France, the first of its kind. It was a race to forget: after ditches, broken axles, lots of breakdowns, he finished tenth, one hundred and twenty hours behind the winner!

The first Gordon Bennett Cup, created by an American billionaire, took place in 1900; it ran from Paris to Lyon, France being at the time the foremost country in terms of numbers of carmakers and cars produced. For Jenatzy, it was a great national cause, defending the Belgian colors. He lined up in a Snoeck. But Charron won in a Panhard & Levassor in only nine hours and nine minutes; that is, traveling at 36.12 mph (57.8 km/h) on average. That was progress. One career fed the other. At the CITA (Compagnie Internationale des Transports Automobiles) in Paris, electric cabs and lorries were built.

Three years later, at the Martini armaments factory at Liège, it was under the name of Jenatzy-Martini that cars inaugurating the use of petrol and electric power were produced; these would have a bright future, eventually. At the same time Camille Jenatzy became one of the pillars of the young Mercedes team, and it was under this rather Spanish-sounding name (in fact that of the daughter of the financier, Emile Jelinek) that the Benz cars raced; they were worried about anti-German feeling among some of their clientele. Jenatzy was a professional driver now. In the aborted 1903 Paris–Madrid race, he came tenth, but later won the most prestigious prize, the Gordon Bennett Cup, and the £8,000 prize money that went with it.

Jenatzy's electric cars lasted a long time, but the man sparkled with ideas. He took out a patent on a magnetic clutch, and carried on with his career, with nothing to promote but his own talent.

The fortune he expected as a minor industrialist, he found thanks to his skill as a driver. In a way it was the victory of passion over reason, of frivolity over seriousness. Being part of the official Mercedes team's baggage train meant

you took part in the most beautiful races—and traveled the world. All year round he prepared and drove in the main European races: France, Belgium, Great Britain, and Italy. And regularly in October, he crossed the Atlantic to race in the Vanderbilt Cup in the New York suburbs, driving enormous cars, which now easily topped 100 mph (160 km/h), though no real progress had been made where braking was concerned. As for road-holding, the steering wheel was now fortunately in overall use: that was definitely a good idea.

He led the life of a paid tourist, a sportsman—rather a happy life, even though his best results were behind him. In 1910, full of experience and wisdom, the Red Devil retired to the Ardennes, to shelter from road accidents.

In 1913, having organized a wild boar hunt for his friends, he decided to imitate the cry of the boar. He did this so well that—seeing the bushes he was concealed behind moving—one of his guests shot at it. Jenatzy was loaded into a Mercedes but, rather ironically, it wasn't fast enough to get him to hospital. He died en route.

The *Jamais Contente* was an example of profiling—if you don't look too closely at the chassis and the driver's body (above, top).

After his record, Jenatzy pursued a career as a racing driver, with cars equipped with a steering wheel, for a change (above, bottom).

Camille du Gast

1868-1942

The Impertinent Amazon

Man invented the car—and then he immediately kept it for himself. But does loving machines necessarily incline you to misogyny? To admit to this would be a betrayal, but to deny it would be hypocrisy.

However, the car's role was to replace physical strength, so it was logical that it should interest women, since men have always let women know how muscularly inferior they are. But it takes a certain temperament to free oneself from social restraints.

The unofficial title of first motorized sportswoman fell to Camille du Gast, born in 1868. This beautiful young woman was twenty-seven years old when her husband, Jules Crespin, the founder of the Dufayel department stores in Paris, died. To her pleasant appearance she added an adventurous character, to which she had already drawn the attention of journalists and the public when she became the first lady parachutist in history, in 1895, despite her family's pleas and even a warning from the authorities. She braved all that and made several tests with the very new system of parachute-weight invented by the Corsican aeronaut, Louis Capazza. She had to go up in the sky to 6,500 feet (2,000 m), then, tearing the envelope of the balloon to simulate a breakdown, come down hanging from just the parachute's canopy. This was in itself a scandal, a sort of fairground exhibition that earned her notoriety and admiration alongside a fair amount of disapproval. Her husband died, leaving her very rich and quite free, with a little daughter. Malicious gossip about her morals continued; it was said she posed naked for the painter Gervex; she had several lovers, including James Gordon Bennett,

the founder of the cup of the same name, awarded at the first annual automobile competition.

In any case, Camille had pursued many other avenues before driving began to interest her. In 1901, she started the Paris–Berlin race at the wheel of a Panhard & Levassor with an impressive engine (7.4 liters), which was covered in flowers from the crowd. Her mechanic was a high-ranking figure: the Prince of Sagan. In Berlin she finished amid ovations, nineteenth out of more than a hundred competitors.

How could she miss *the* event of the time: the 1903 Paris–Madrid race, which had already been proclaimed the race of the century? The start saw her perched in her lofty de Dietrich racer, rigged out against the dust and speed (highs of 75 mph/120 km/h), all without a windscreen. Of course she was wearing a dress, but she had made a hat with several flaps in order to protect her face as much as possible. In one session, without incident and well positioned, she covered the first 350 miles (550 km), mudguard to mudguard with Stead, who was driving a car like hers. But when she tried to overtake Salleron (driving a Mors), Stead bumped into her and his car abruptly left the road, throwing the mechanic out and rolling onto its unfortunate driver. The "guilty party," Salleron, was already miles away in a cloud of dust and quite unaware of the accident he had caused. Seeing the seriousness of the

Photography was also a new art. Here, Camille du Gast poses, in the latest fashions, under magnesium lamps, in front of a neoclassical set (facing page).

Course Paris-Berlin.
Madame Camille Crespin du Gast vient de faire peser sa
Voiture "Panhard" à l'Automobile-Club.

On the Place de la
Concorde, Camille
du Gast had no need
to worry about traffic
jams. At the starting
line, her car was covered
with flowers.

incident, Camille du Gast stopped, sacrificing her race. This chivalrous gesture in itself was quite normal at the time, but what was more surprising to both the mechanics were the young woman's calm and physical dedication, which were a great help in getting the heavy car turned over and getting Stead out.

The race turned into a catastrophe: there were numerous accidents—many fatal—and it was halted at Bordeaux. The following year, Camille put herself in for the heats in the Gordon Bennett cup. It was country racing against country; it was a sort of world cup of driving and technique. Some competitors considered the presence of a woman driver unsuitable. Although there was no incident on the course that she could be reproached with, the authorities were called upon in the name of good moral standards to intervene and they forbade her from taking part, "to avoid the risks of her feminine nervousness." This was of course a ridiculous decision, made by a few mustachioed, sideburn-sporting officials and against which she naturally appealed, but to no avail. For Camille du Gast it was the end of the road, at least as far as cars were concerned, but she continued to pursue speed in the form of motorboats, with just as much enthusiasm and defiance.

"I pulled down the two flaps on my cap and I was ready, protected from the wind and the dust."

Louis Renault

1877-1944

Ascension

When a new industry is born there's always a very interesting moment of hesitancy: yesterday's whim is in the process of becoming tomorrow's big business. In a few years, Louis Renault, an introspective youngster seeking refuge in his mechanical hobbies, became one of the country's top entrepreneurs.

On December 24, 1898, the penultimate Christmas of the century, Louis Renault, twenty-one years old, already quite definitely preferred oil and grease and dirt to anything else. He had built a "workshop," almost a cabin for himself, deep in the grounds of the villa where his mother and two brothers, rich haberdashers in Paris, lived at weekends. It was an out-of-the-way place and it was this timid young man's lair. He was not very sociable, and felt uncomfortable with his own family; their commercial success and moneyed background gave them a certain social standing, and being at ease in society was—for them— essential to success. Since his teenage years, since the death of his father, young Louis had piled up experience and skills round a forge in which he made the simple and more sophisticated parts of a marvel: his first little car, the *voiturette*.

The car, as an idea, was on everybody's lips, but the theory had yet to translate into a widespread reality. Hundreds of little craftsmen among the hansom cab and bicycle-makers were producing a few examples every year. There were steam omnibuses, petrol-engined tricycles, and a few heavy cars that were very expensive to run and to buy. But Louis had got this little car to work, and his brother Marcel, five years his senior, invited him to celebrate at the Christmas

Eve party he was throwing for his friends at a restaurant on the Place de Clichy.

Louis parked his car in front of the restaurant. The *voiturette* was only 6 ft. 3 in. (1.90 m) long, 2 ft. (60 cm) shorter than a present-day Smart car. Its engine was rated at just ¾ bhp. But the machine did have four wheels, like the big cars, and a three-gear transmission, the third being directly geared to the engine, a simple and solid invention in those days when transmission for a lot of cars still used a chain, like bikes.

Marcel's friends were rich and happy and made fun of him. Louis was proud to show off the *voiturette*'s qualities, betting it could go up Rue Lepic, the steep slope on Montmartre, which was just as hard on pedestrians as it was on horses. He took one of the guests, who returned enchanted, then another and then another. That Christmas Eve, the Renault *voiturette* climbed the slope twelve times and the next morning Renault had his first twelve orders! His older brothers suddenly took his hobby seriously, reckoning that it could bring in more money than haberdashery did. For Louis, real life had just begun.

His first twelve customers had put down their deposits in cash, but this disturbed Louis. This sum represented a small fortune for a young

Louis Renault at fifty (facing page). His factories were producing thirty thousand cars every year.

Between 1898 and 1914, Renault built a huge company, learning as he went along. One of the first advertisements for Renault Frères (far left), and serried rows of the "Victory Tank" (left).

man, but it was far from being enough to set up a factory. Marcel and Fernand, however, pragmatic and well versed in business mores, put together 60,000 francs and founded the company Renault Frères, which was to exploit the "Louis Renault systems." From February 9, 1899, Louis patented direct meshing. Other people had worked it out, each in his own shed, but Louis was the first to patent it and it became a large source of profit in the immediate future.

At the same time, at 7 Place des Victoires, they opened a sales office, where Marcel and Fernand took orders. The family property at Billancourt, at 119 Rue Point-du-Jour, was pompously christened "the factory." Louis turned out to be formidable as a team leader, imperious but putting his all into the business; he knew how to surround himself with swift and efficient colleagues. Renault Frères was born: workforce, six people.

The *voiturette* was the "masterpiece" by this moody, quick-tempered, and meticulous scion. It became the prototype for an industrial venture; its simplicity enabled it to be reproduced at a rate that other, much more business-hardened craftsmen had trouble matching. At the same time, the Renaults started taking over Billancourt property.

At first a boat hangar was annexed to honor the first twelve orders. At the same time, in France alone, dozens of the same type of artisan ventures started up. But during 1900, Renault produced and sold seventy-six cars. And two years later, there were four hundred employees producing two hundred and ninety cars!

Renault changed from an artisan's workshop, fragile yet bold, into a young, inventive, and prosperous company. At the same this family venture was taking off, so was the whole idea of

the car. France was, with Germany, the foremost car producer: Billancourt vibrated next to a world center. Paris was a base for races: Paris-Trouville, Paris-Ostend, Paris-Vienna; and these were triumphs for Renault. The catalog got bigger, the cars got bigger, and Renault now produced its own engines. The Renaults obviously took part in races, to test the worth of their machines, to convince a clientele with dozens of French and foreign makes to chose from. By December 1901, all 1902's production had already been sold. They raced the cars for the fun and interest also; at the steering wheel it was either Louis or Marcel, the former button merchant who was enthusiastic about his brother's machines. This was the best period: sporting successes made life easy, Louis's ideas and his ability to run the workshop made him a boss and a leader, and he had a business which worked really well, had succeeded in getting the world moving; it was enough to thrill a young man of twenty-five.

The 1903 Paris–Madrid, the "race of the century"— already!—was advertised all over the place, attracting competitors from all over the world. Tens of thousands of spectators traveled from Paris to Versailles to witness the start. A huge crowd coming by car, bike, or special train, or even on foot, crowded in front of the chateau gates where the cars, the monarchs of that era, were being waved off. Two hundred and twenty-one competitors started every minute from 03.45 a.m. onwards.

Louis and Marcel drove machines which had been specially designed for the event: a powerful, thundering 6.3-liter four-cylinder engine with the famous Renault gearbox and an insect's silhouette. No roof or windscreen to protect the driver and his mechanic; the bodywork was reduced to a hooked bonnet, one of the make's features, flanked by two radiators on the sides which warped the air around them. The machine barely weighed 1,430 lb. (650 kg) and sped along at 88 mph (140 km/h). All that with the crudest of brakes, on beaten earth roads with bends only designed for the speed of a horse cart, with hump-backed bridges which were so arched they threatened to scrape the undersides of the machines and to throw them up into the air as if from trampolines. And the dust, that enemy, the huge cloud which told his pursuers where each competitor was. But how on earth could you get any nearer when you couldn't see anything? How did you overtake? The boldest didn't look at the road, but steered by looking at the tops of the trees, planted on the edge of the road to provide shade for walkers, whose trunks threatened to kill any clumsy drivers. Before Orleans, Louis had gained six minutes and overtaken all the rivals who had left before him. He reached Bordeaux, breaking the record: 60.62 mph (97 km/h) on average, on earthen roads and almost without brakes. Some driving. At the same time he learned where he was in the race and he learned that his brother Marcel had gone off the road. He was

injured and dying. Louis set off back to where the accident had occurred. In fact the Paris–Madrid race had been stopped by the government at Bordeaux. There'd been too many accidents. In Spain the crowds, just as enthusiastic as in France, were expecting to greet the heroes; the cancellation of the race caused riots. But all this was immaterial to Louis. Marcel was dead, and Louis never raced again.

Despite the family's personal tragedy, the Renault victories caused an avalanche of orders. Automobiles had to be made. In 1910, the factory (which had now fully earned that title) already occupied more than 500,000 sq. ft. (46,500 sq. m) and employed 3,200 people, running about under the severe leadership of young Mr. Louis. In August 1914, the factory closed down, but at the very last minute, the government realized that Private Renault would be more useful behind the lines. The cauldron at the front had to be supplied with shells and trucks. So 1914 saw the factory surface area and the workforce triple, bursting the walls and production capacity. Renault bought up and shared out land in the

Enthusiastic onlookers greeted the different stages of the 1903 Paris–Madrid. Everything was new: bikes, tires, cars, and photographs. The road itself was made for horse-drawn carts, though.

same way that automobiles were then being built: on a production line. The pressure was such that the buildings were often of poor quality. In 1916, a building collapsed, killing sixty workers.

From 1917 onward it was the Renault light tank, designed by Louis in person, which contributed to the German defeat. The Renault factories had deserved their country's praise; they had also hoarded unequalled profits.

War had changed men, those who survived it. Workers' theories had become structured and the example of the Russian revolution had vulgarized the notion of "capitalist." With his timid person's scorn and his arrogance, with his position as the country's foremost industrialist, with his practice of production rates which he brought in after visiting Ford, the American, Louis Renault was a fairly good caricature for the workers. This mechanic boss, this man with the dirty nails, soon came to be known as the "Ogre of Billancourt" (a title taken from the newspaper L'Humanité) because of his intransigence. Other dreams, collective ones, now opposed his own. It must be said that the Renault factories were in no way leisure centers, and that Renault, like Citroën, was a flamboyant boss and a big spender. His private life got him talked about; he was almost officially bigamous, housing wife and mistress in the same private house on the Avenue Foch. For a long time Chryséis, his river yacht equipped with two enormous Renault engines, was tied up in front of the factory.

The factory got bigger, to the limits of what was possible. Renault had his eye on Seguin Island (in the Seine), which was in front of his property. But it was so low that to avoid the river in spate, it had to be covered with a 211,680,000 cu. ft. (600,000 cu. m) concrete "plinth" before building could be started. One parcel of land resisted the industrialist's pressure and offers; it belonged to a family of diehards, the Gallice family, whose son had been killed in 1918 in a Renault tank.

But in the end Louis Renault got hold of it all. The factory looked like an aircraft carrier, a completed artifact except for four poplars remaining at the bows of the ship and four at the stern. In the forward point he installed the compressed air factory (for Renault made its own fluids), the assembly plant for the locomotives (for Renault made trains, and planes, and trucks)

and below, in the basement, was the test track, the paved bowels of the company where every car was driven, just after assembly, to test if everything was all right.

Renault's dream was to be self-sufficient. He disdained banks as much as possible. And on his cars he made everything: bodywork, spark plugs, carburetors, starters, and even upholstery, and bonnets. The metal structure of the new buildings had been cast in his own forges at Bas Meudon. The bricks of the walls were made from sand that had already served to cast the engine and gearbox casings. The factory manholes proudly bear the name Renault.

As World War II broke out, the factories were in full production; they were put under German control and produced for Germany, as did factories throughout the rest of France. All the bosses were questioned after the war and some of them had indeed resisted, sabotaged, and slowed down production. Renault hadn't. Could he even wittingly formulate the notion of working badly? "His" factory had been bombed. On March 3, 1942, 460 tons of English bombs had been dropped; there were 500 dead and Seguin was shattered. Renault rebuilt it. On April 4, 1943, 118 tons of American bombs fell and Marcel's monument was razed to the ground. Renault rebuilt everything. Picard, one of his closest colleagues, remarked dryly: "Accusing him of liking the Germans? That's crazy! He didn't like anybody!"

Renault was arrested and imprisoned; his factory was requisitioned, under state tutelage, and then nationalized. A month later, Louis died. Foreign historians who have studied the horrors of the collaboration and the blunders made during the French Liberation nowadays agree that beatings and a lack of care led to his death. There's still an enduring doubt: was Louis Renault "simply" treated like thousands of other people in those days which were so favorable to all sorts of exactions, or was it a deliberate crime? He died on October 24, 1944, avoiding a trial in which he might have been allowed to be defended.

Before the war, Renault created mass-produced automobiles and small series of luxury cars. Here, a Nervasport Cabriolet is demonstrated in the grounds at Saint-Cloud (facing page).

Jules Bonnot
1876-1912

The Gangster in a Car

A confirmed, vicious, unscrupulous, and ruthless criminal—it's difficult to admit you could ever be fascinated by such a pure evildoer. However, Bonnot was a man who took orders from nobody else, who invented his own way of making France quake, and did it well.

The expression "gangsters in a car" appeared in the newspapers on December 22, 1911, on the day following the murder of an assistant cashier in the Rue Ordener in Paris, at the entrance to a branch of the Société Générale Bank, which for that matter still exists. The facts were these. A man, Garnier, suddenly approached the employee, shot him twice with a revolver, tore his bag from him, then dived into a parked car, which immediately sped off. Bonnot had remained at the wheel.

"Anarchists!" was the verdict of the newspapers. The job in the Rue Ordener set off a crimewave which was indeed the action of a gang determined to put the theory of the "*reprise individuelle*"—"individual reclamation" (that is, theft as a means of reappropriating wealth)—to more profitable use. Bonnot was among them, though he wasn't the Ravachol or Kropotkin type; he wasn't a depraved intellectual, but at first a radicalized worker, then a determined thug. The gang was named after him, although he was neither its leader (the brains behind the jobs was Raymond Callemin, dubbed "Raymond la Science"), nor its first killer (that was Octave Garnier), but because he was most often the driver. The driver earned the prestige; without him, nothing was possible. Bonnot was above all else a technician, a confirmed mechanic and a skilled driver; he had even been a chauffeur in London in the service of one Arthur Conan Doyle. The creator of Sherlock Holmes turned out to be a bit short on intuition and deduction, and had no inkling as to his servant's destiny.

Although anarchist ideas influenced him when he returned to Paris, he was the one who probably had the idea of using a car. He was merely being pragmatic: the getaway would be quicker and the hold-up would have a better chance of succeeding. But it was actually all much simpler than that: Bonnot could not do without a car. The powerful Delaunay-Belleville used in the Rue Ordener job was found at Dieppe only a few hours later. This discovery highlighted the extraordinary mobility that the car now offered bandits, and made the public tremble. The problem was that the police themselves were still on foot or on horse, or even on bicycles.

That ability of evildoers seemingly to be everywhere had turned from nameless fear into something tangible: if Dieppe was now effectively little farther than a Paris suburb, the gangsters could be anywhere. The whole population was looking askance at its neighbors and a flood of denunciations (up to seven hundred letters a day) poured into police stations.

A snapshot of Jules Bonnot (facing page), taken by the criminal records office and reproduced in the newspapers under suitable labels: the "monster," the "anarchist," and the "bandit in a car."

Before each job, a car had to be found. Killing the driver and shooting the occupants at point-blank range hardly seemed to trouble them. On some occasions, they would just take a taxi to the corner of a wood, throw pepper in the driver's eyes and leave him to walk back. But to make sure they had the best cars and therefore the surest way of being able to get away quickly, it was better to get hold of one from the garage next to a bourgeois home.

The gang could blame Bonnot for making one driving mistake when crossing Paris at the wheel of another Delaunay-Belleville. It had been stolen for a job planned for the following day at Villeneuve-Saint-Georges. Bonnot cut foolishly across a roundabout in front of the Gare Saint-Lazare and was brought to a halt by a horsedrawn omnibus which was turning off. No doubt he couldn't be patient like everybody else and remain in the queue. There was the sound of a whistle and one of those poor policemen whom Bonnot hated so much came up. Bonnot tried to get away from him by just driving away, but the cop managed to jump onto the running board and Callemin (or perhaps Garnier?) shot him dead. This almost gratuitous, purely violent act against society counted for a lot in the morbid fascination that the Bonnot mob exerted on the public right up to the end.

Was it really morbid fascination? Yes. A few holdups later, when Bonnot had been tracked down,

the siege of the house lasted almost two days. As the hours went by, reinforcements arrived and a huge crowd gathered. The troops had been brought in, and each time they—or the police—attacked, Bonnot's mob responded with sustained gunfire. Each time the explosive experts got close—they went as far as to blow up the house—the crowd applauded, happy to see this free show and this instant justice. That was enough to endorse these individualists and outlaws, who scorned the public authorities just as much as they did democracy.

Bonnot—the Quick, the Uncatchable, the Driver—met his end there and then, stuck in a loft, rolled up between two mattresses, protecting himself from the bullets tearing through the slum house walls. His death wasn't without a certain grandeur, in the end. He had already drawn up his "will," as he wanted to clear the names of his anarchist sympathizers and to prevent the police from confusing them with his mob.

In Bonnot's wake, other "public enemies" also used the car as a getaway method; some of them even turned them into assault vehicles, into rams. Today it has become commonplace. But when Bonnot was behaving so ruthlessly, many a bourgeois must have trembled under his bedclothes at the sound of a six-cylinder car passing beneath his windows at full speed.

The "Bonnot Gang": in fact they were rebels caught up in strategic terrorism and individual action, to the great annoyance of the pacifist anarchist theoreticians.

L'automobile volée puis abandonnée par les criminels

L'automobile volée par les bandits sur la route de Montgeron, une fois leur premier crime accompli, est une 18-chevaux bleu foncé, aux filets jaunes, munie de deux phares et de deux res, elle fut entourée toute la journée par une foule nombreuse.

lanternes. Dans la poursuite que livra la police aux malfaiteurs, ceux-ci abandonnèrent la voiture à Asnières pour sauter dans un train. Garée en face du commissariat de police d'Asniè-

1. LA FOULE ENTOURE L'AUTO DU CRIME, A ASNIÈRES. — 2. M. BERTILLON (A) ET LE COMMISSAIRE DE POLICE D'ASNIÈRES, M. KAYRAL (B), PRENANT LES EMPREINTES DES DOIGTS DES MALFAITEURS. — 3. L'INTÉ-

The stolen Delaunay-Belleville, abandoned after the attack, illustrated in a contemporary newspaper account (left) and being examined (below). There was an open-air compartment for the driver and the valet, and a closed-in, velvet-lined one for the owners.

Jules Goux
1885-1965

When Jules is Driving

A combustion engine, especially a racing engine, is a box
of fireworks, or a cauldron bubbling over with mysteries,
which end up as noise and speed. Riding one is an adventure.
Designing one is too. Jules Goux lived out both these adventures.

Jules Goux was married to Peugeot. His father was one of the managers in the bicycle division. He himself studied at the Arts et Métiers with a view to becoming a draftsman, an aim he reached in 1903 aged eighteen, with Peugeot, of course. There he dealt with motorbikes, racing ones if he could, and also riding them. And from there to the car; they had only two more wheels and Jules Goux was ready for any adventure that his era could offer. Besides, becoming the official driver did not prevent him in his spare moments from designing and building a plane, which he then promptly crashed. With his colleague, teammate, rival, and buddy Georges Boillot, they bought a Blériot on which they inflicted the same fate. Apparently they had more talent for moving about on land, which at the time meant traveling at roughly the same speed, and they devoted themselves to it full time. On the work side, they won the races their boss wanted in the *voiturettes* category.

Envying the big machines, which were much more exciting to drive, and wanting to take part in world-class races, they decided to build their own car.

To climb the speed ladder, you need a few tightrope artists who don't suffer from a fear of heights. When improving a record, these acrobats show a prowess in the face of what might appear to be the prospect of certain death that inspires only animal-like fear among everyone else. It's like the mountaineer who opens a way up a rock face: it won't seem so glorious after he has finished; every so often he leaves a few pitons to mark out the difficulties for those who will never be anything other than followers.

Jules Goux and Georges Boillot forged their friendship at Lion-Peugeot. Despite the very French influence present in the races at the time, and to which Goux and Boillot seemed to be quite sensitive, the sportsman's international already existed, like a sort of club which, although it respected flags, disdained frontiers: a French driver would have more in common with his Italian, American, or German counterparts than with the manager employing him. Goux and Boillot made friends with the Italian Paolo Zuccarelli, who defended Hispano-Suiza's colors, though Goux would never have thought of making any sort of progress without driving "his" make.

Robert Peugeot, who ran the firm, had a feeling that these two lads would be able to produce something interesting, so he gave them a free hand, an almost under-the-table "research budget," and a separate workshop at Suresnes. When the regular engineers, engaged in the more worthy but less exciting job of keeping everyday

Jules Goux (facing page):
simply one of the best
drivers of his time.
The sheer size of the
Peugeot's steering wheel
gives an idea of the
sweeping movements
needed to steer it.

Peugeots on the road, learned of this they were understandably annoyed. They nicknamed the little team of mad-keen engineer-drivers "the Charlatans," and it stuck.

Indeed Goux wasn't an engineer, but when you drove these strange little grasshoppers, the echo of their vibrations and penalizing inertia could be felt throughout your whole body. A driver is in a position to talk about mechanics, rather as a wine-taster can talk about chemistry: without ever learning it but by experiencing it, by making "tasting" a specialization, and by making the senses highly attuned. All the same, Jules Goux and Georges Boillot and Paolo Zuccarelli took on the services of a Swiss industrial draftsman, Ernest Henri.

It was true that these four musketeers did foster a brotherhood of eccentrics, even going so far as to conclude a pact which would flummox our modern Grand Prix paddocks, where you can't smell the oil, grease, and dirt any more, but instead a pervading smell of pig manure. With the Charlatans, bonuses and winnings were shared out four ways. As for rewarding the best inventor among them, it was agreed that each discovery would be rewarded by a meal paid for by the other three.

The Peugeot L76 came straight from the Charlatans' reflections; the musty engineers made fun of it but it did mean a real technical leap forward. Hemispheric combustion chamber, four valves per cylinder, desmodromic controls.... Don't change anything: ninety-five years later it still describes a very beautiful engine; 148 bhp at 2,000 rpm, 120 mph. As for the rest, don't let's dream: they didn't invent the brakes, or the really rigid chassis, or no-puncture tires. The L76 was brought out and presented just before the 1912 ACF Grand Prix, which Boillot won driving it.

On April 12, 1913, traveling at 106.25 mph (170 km/h), Goux beat the world hour record, held until then by a plane! The 3-liter version won the Côte du Ventoux race (Boillot), the French Grand Prix (Paolo Zuccarelli), and the *Auto Magazine* Cup (Jules Goux), which all consecrated the Charlatans' worth. It was a busy spring and they still had to cross the Atlantic.

At the beginning of the twentieth century in the United States, gigantism and modernity went hand in hand with any human dream. The conquest of the West wasn't even over before people started making it into a show for those living in the East. Giant triple marquee circuses crisscrossed the country. It was of course in America that the French invention, the cinema, originally more of a technical and fairground curiosity, started becoming the leading show industry in the world.

Naturally the ambition of the Indianapolis Grand Prix organizers was to make it the biggest race in the world. It was a race towards a hugeness that combated and at the same time highlighted the country's profound provincialism prior to 1914. Permanent structures, an a priori perfect brick track, huge prizes, qualification trials spread out over weeks, 500 mile-long race and a date chosen without any complexes: Independence Day. The circuit was a ring with cambered bends to obtain the highest speeds possible, since it was those figures that interested the public most. This speed ring was the purest dream of an infinitely straight line, but closed in, in full sight of the stands: a stylized vision of racing, quite different from that seen in Europe.

In each car there were two people, the driver and the mechanic; it was a matter of trusting each other.

It was devilishly hot, continentally hot, and the huge stands were full. Jules Goux started cheekily in the lead. Tire problems quickly made him lose his place, but it wasn't anything serious, the race was a long one. There was no question of racing flat out blindly, as you might expect: each bend was subtly different and presupposed a different approach and way of slowing down. This was a quest for pure speed, tightly controlled, cultivated to within a tenth of a second; this was when driving was at its most cerebral, where physical courage—which is a more positive variant of nervous tension—gave way to the discipline of willpower.

The driver has to build himself a cold determination, to gainsay any reasonable calculation of danger, increased and regenerated by the length of the race. After the eighteenth lap, Zuccarelli's engine broke its crankshaft. During the fifty-first lap, Jack Tower's Duesenberg (which had made the best average during the trials), took the southwest bend badly, rolled over immediately, and threw out the two men. Tower broke a leg, his mechanic broke some ribs. Goux went on round tirelessly. You had to hold out for 500 miles, going round and round for more than six hours. Back in the lead, Goux didn't wait for the finish to break open his champagne. When he stopped mid-race to change his rear tires, he also proceeded

Jules Goux during the 1912 Sarthe Grand Prix. He is driving one of the cars he designed with the "Charlatans" team.

to reload his personal supply of brut champagne, brought in on purpose.

During the two hundredth and last lap, Merz's Stutz caught fire. This didn't stop Merz, though, and he completed the last kilometers belching flames and smoke, but grabbed the third place.

The day had been beautiful, the race epic, and the unexpected victory for the Peugeot and Jules Goux finished it off perfectly. Unfortunately, although there was good feedback in Europe, Peugeot was not able to make good its fame in the United States because there was not enough time before the outbreak of war in 1914.

When you are an innovator, it is strange how people first rebel against your ideas or make fun of you, and then become enthusiastic for them, which by dint of being so successful have become quite logical. Of course, the Charlatans' personal successes were very quickly embraced by their former rivals with Peugeot and in the United States, the influence of the magical four-cylinder engine went so far that a line of racing engines was created which, under the name of first Miller, and then Offenhauser, dominated the Indianapolis 500 until 1960. Jules Goux could laugh every year at this postscript to their

exploits. He was the last of the three Charlatans to disappear, in 1965. Paolo Zuccarelli, barely back from that glorious trip stateside, was killed when he ran into a carriage while scouting out the 1913 ACF Grand Prix route. He was twenty-seven. As for Georges Bolliot, basking in the glory of a second consecutive win in the French Grand Prix, he fought in the air force and was killed on May 20, 1916 when he attacked five Fokkers single-handed—still that thirst for records.

Henry Ford

1863–1947

The Man from Detroit

The year was 1863 and the cliché about the new world, America, was absolutely true. Buildings were sprouting up every other day, immigrants were crowding in, and companies were being created all over the place; they prospered or disappeared in a few weeks. And it was there in Dearborn, Michigan, that Henry Ford came into the world, that world.

Henry's father, William, had emigrated from Ireland in 1847. After two years enduring bitter, deadly famine, he crossed the sea for a new territory, where arable land was available in large quantities. America.

Little Henry grew like the local maize, quickly and strong, but lacked sophistication. In this fast-moving environment, he fidgeted more than anybody else. He couldn't bear going to school; even his most fervent admirers, and there were plenty of them, had to admit that he was never able to express himself in a polished style, or even master elementary writing; nor could he stand working in the fields, which he found so physically punishing, and above all so slow. On the other hand, he did lots of different jobs: apprentice in a steam engine company, foundry worker, basic mechanic, and farm machines salesman; in these pursuits he was skillful and interested in anything new.

At twenty-five, he married Clara Bryant ("the most important day in my life," he was to say later) and settled in Detroit, the big town nearest to Dearborn. He was about thirty and had made himself indispensable at Edison's; the shareholders even offered him the job of managing director, but on one condition—they thought it a minor one: that he stop tinkering with smelly and noisy petrol-engined machines in that shed of his, as this seemed quite unsuitable for somebody who was supposed to be promoting electricity. Ford knew that his "tinkering" was the cornerstone of his ambition, and by 1903 he'd in fact managed to find shareholders to help him found the Ford Motor Company. The fruit of his labors was indeed inside that shed: it was an automobile machine. It was a matter of impressing his partners then the customers; potentially there would be a lot of them because the real aim was to produce a car for everyone. But where cars were concerned, other models were beginning to appear on the market, and for him to be convincing, his had to be really special—very fast, for example. The Henry Ford Company (which he'd founded in 1901), thought this digression a waste of time: Henry left the company (it became the Cadillac Motor Company) in order to try and start again, this time with more independence.

The flagship model was christened Ford 999 after a record-breaking locomotive. Given the size of the machine, a 19-liter four-cylinder engine, it wasn't a bad find. The car was as spectacular as it was basic: a huge vertical radiator, a very big

Henry Ford, Sr. (facing page). A self-made man with rigid ideas and an iron will, he remains one of America's best-known figures and the first true car industrialist.

The Ford factories in Detroit during World War I. A fleet of ambulances stands ready to leave for the front (above).
The first workshops (right).
A few colleagues (obviously junior) and a keen will to succeed.

Early days: the Ford 999's bare chassis with a huge 19-liter, four-cylinder engine. In 1904, Henry Ford himself (standing at right in photo) broke the 100 miles an hour barrier at its wheel.

engine and a bare chassis on which there was a seat. Ford installed a cycling champion first, then eventually took over the joystick (there wasn't any steering wheel) himself and reached his goal: to bring the absolute world speed record—91.37 mph (just over 147 km/h) in 1904—to America. For that record Henry Ford would now be inscribed forever on the international roll of history. This next attempt to raise capital was a real success. The name Ford became a true brand, bringing in more than 300 percent profits in the first year for its shareholders.

"Mr. Ford's" intuitions were no longer challenged. They went from model to model (in alphabetical order), chasing his vision: a car that was so cheap that anybody could buy it, including—and this is where the idea was so significant—those who made it. The answer was the "T" Model, brought to London to underline its universal appeal. Ford had kept it simple: one transversal spring per axle, no differential, two gears only, lubricated by gravity (i.e. the oil fell, drop by drop, like mayonnaise) onto the part to be oiled, and high wheels to run over all the ruts.

This was in 1908, and Ford's career could have stopped there: he had just introduced the car of his dreams, which was going to get America on its wheels. More than 16.5 million were built up to 1927, without any major changes except for those necessary to satisfy the incessant requirements of rationalization. In 1908, it took fifteen men twelve hours to build one car; from 1914, only nine

workers were needed, taking just one and a half hours. When production moved to the assembly line, the T was painted black only because it was the quickest-drying paint—his customers could have "any color . . . so long as it's black."

As for the rest, the Ford Motor Company was run along similar hare-brained lines, with the principles of domestic economy exaggerated to the point of obsession. At least Henry Ford's vertiginous business success could comfort him in his belief that his principles were right, even if they were not at all traditional.

In the name of independence he refused to accept the idea of paying his shareholders any dividends and, when the courts forced him to, he almost ruined himself by buying up all the shares. In the name of pacifism, and with real concern for the public good, he announced publicly that he would not collect the profits made on the 1917–18 war production (vehicles, plane engines, and helmets). In the name of simplicity, he refused to allow his only son, Edsel, to carry out any overambitious developments for the Ford T, like fitting windscreen wipers. But at the same time, and in the name of progress, he wore out his research team in futile studies for an X-shaped engine.

Some of his decisions took on crusade-like proportions. To cut the price of natural rubber, which the English monopolized with their Malayan plantations, he founded Fordlandia on the River Amazon, set up his managers there (they were engineers rather than horticulturists), planted huge numbers of hevea plants (but much too close to each other so that soon they were diseased), imposed the same regulations as in his factories (including no smoking, in the fields or even in the accommodation, and hours which were totally unsuited to equatorial climates). The workers rebelled, the managers fled in a boat protected by the Brazilian army and the town was abandoned—a complete fiasco.

In an atttempt to fight Communism, he managed to persuade the Soviet government to build a factory at Nijni-Novgorod, hoping to "invade the Russians with capitalism." Meanwhile, considering his own destiny and success to be exemplary, he published several books of enlightenment and moral support. One of them, the *International Jew*, full of the most inept anti-Semitic precepts, was read and admired as far away as the Munich prisons by one Adolf Hitler. Ford was also terribly intransigent, haunted by the perils of laziness and the cult of cost pricing, and therefore of productivity. After 1929, he fought an almost open war against the trades unions, keeping up a militia of vigilantes to watch over the production lines, installing redoubts at his factory entrances to discourage the strikers' assaults.

On a more private note, it seemed to be extremely difficult for him to allow his son to run the company. Although Edsel had officially held the reins since 1919, he could only smooth the edges of the rough paths that the patriarch brutally hacked out. When Edsel suddenly died in 1943, felled by cancer, Henry went back to work, much to the despair of his board of directors. As a result, without Edsel's soothing influence, the conflict with the trades unions flared up again; marketing was neglected whereas what the situation needed was tact and foresight. So much so that for a while the Roosevelt government envisaged nationalizing the company, but finally decided to free Edsel's young son from his military obligations so that he could turn the company around.

Henry Ford had an exceptional destiny, both brilliant and somber; here was the contrasted picture of a man who was both blind and visionary, for although there was the occasional swerve, there is no doubt that above all Henry Ford liked to steer his own life himself. It appears that he saw the world as a set of specifications, with simple springs and willpower as its raw material. What was complex eluded him completely, and his good sense led him into very bad habits. But he never looked so smiling, so friendly as when he was driving one of his cars; it was as though while he was driving towards the photographer, he was offering him a present. That present was what Ford couldn't stop thinking of as the marvel of the century: the car. And he himself was the man who had most contributed to its boom.

The Ford Motor Company survived its founder to become one of the three big American makers. Here, Marilyn Monroe is pictured in a 1956 Thunderbird.

A masterpiece of simplicity and symbol of the company: the Model T Ford. Built on the first assembly lines from 1908 to 1927: 16 million of them and all of them black. The Tin Lizzie got the United States mobile.

Between Two Wars

Nymphs and Titans

The car had come of age. Its progress, at the expense—and for the benefit—of thousands of companies, transformed society. It had proved its qualities, its suitability in all conditions; it had been realized in numerous ways: vans, market wagons, seductresses, travelers, and racers. And it had even done its military service, as command cars, armored cars, troop transports, ambulances. But still it hadn't settled down. The engineers thought they were prophets, the racing drivers still thought they were archangels, the happy customers Phaetons who had borrowed the Sun's chariot. The car was still magical, almost allowing man the possibility of being in several places at the same time; giving him the ability to steer clear of that old inevitability: slowness. It was the Roaring Twenties, and the car, which was becoming more and more widespread, took part in this madness.

Fritz von Opel
Joel Woolf Barnato
André Derain
Jean Bugatti
Hellé Nice
Tazio Nuvolari
Alfred Neubauer
Blaise Cendrars
Robert Benoist

Fritz von Opel
1899-1971

The Human Cannonball

A few daredevils lurked behind some of the original car names, settling down just in time to profit industrially and commercially from the notoriety they acquired by their boldness and courage. As for those who were lucky enough to have the same name as a famous car, they tended to manage their heritage much more calmly.

When Fritz von Opel became interested in the RAK project in 1928, the firm that bore his name was already sixty years old (RAK stood for *Rakettenprogramm*, or rocket program). His grandfather, Adam, had founded the company, first to make sewing machines in 1863, then bicycles from 1886. By the 1920s, Opel was the world's foremost maker of bicycles. You might say that Fritz wasn't frightened of "getting on his bike" to earn a living.

From 1899, the Opel firm started making quite good tourism and racing cars, which Fritz himself sometimes drove in races. But meanwhile there was another, completely separate mechanical adventure that a certain Jules Verne-like figure, Max Valier, had asked him to back. Valier had coolly invented the rocket engine. And Fritz was extremely interested in his work.

A production series Opel was given a profiled body and fitted with a battery of twelve rockets. The test driver took the wheel of the RAK. The first attempt, short but smoky, proved that the system worked. When ignited, the machine was indeed propelled forwards; that was a relief, since it had not actually been taken for granted. The speed of 62.5 mph (100 km/h), reached eight seconds after the off, had only been maintained for a few seconds before the rockets ran out of powder and the monster, suddenly silent, coasted to a halt. In terms of acceleration, there was no doubt it had worked. The whole point of the rocket was that it pushed against air and did not need to transmit its power to drive the wheels, which would then spin, dispersing the power, with a smell of burning rubber from the over-narrow tires (nobody had yet had the idea of widening them to increase road-holding). A car powered by rockets presented advantages that were worth exploring. Obviously there was no question of traveling like that, but for setting a record, why not? At any rate there was some publicity to made there.

A month later, on May 23, 1928, Fritz himself lined up the prototype RAK-2 on the Avus track in the Berlin suburbs. This was an extraordinary autodrome, entirely given over to speed. The track was made up of two straight lines, each 6 miles (10 km) long, joined by two cambered bends like a velodrome. Von Opel knew the place well; with one of his cars, a much more standard model than this one, he had won the 1921 inaugural race. Before starting the afternoon's attraction, which promised

She won first prize for elegance at Bournemouth in 1928. So young and so sweet, and her car was a Ballot (p. 40).

His round glasses made him look more like Professor Calculus than a speed hero. In fact, von Opel had a bit of both in him (facing page).

to be brief, Fritz made a farsighted philanthropist's speech, very much in the spirit of the times. "Today we want to test the maximum speed the human body can take. We are here on the threshold of a new era: soon man will travel in space. Imagine the day when the first manned rocket with our beautiful country's name on its fuselage, will go round the earth faster than even the sun!"

Whereupon Gagarin's forerunner pulled down his thick goggles and, bareheaded, perhaps so that he would be recognizable on the photos and films ordered for the occasion, he climbed into the machine's single seat (no passenger had thought it wise to ask for an extra seat). This time there weren't twelve but twenty-four rockets installed behind the driver.

The rockets were lit. In the noise of the explosion, the car shot away, like a "jack" jumping out of its box, leaving only a cloud of white smoke in front of the spectators' eyes. It reached the fabulous speed of 143.75 mph (230 km/h).

The acceleration was not measured very accurately, nor were the G forces that went with it; but Fritz's deformed face, as if pulled backwards, gave a good idea of the sensations he must have felt. As for the spectators, who had had the idea of waiting for the machine a bit further on, they were dumbfounded: the car sped past them with its wheels rearing up! A journalist noted that: "One extra rocket and this mad project would have sent its inventor to the grave. The vehicle flew past the track rather than along it." There's no point in emphasizing the fact that not even the best driver could have chosen his trajectory under those conditions; looking back it makes you shudder.

Never mind, von Opel got the RAK-3 started. To avoid having to worry about steering, the vehicle was placed on rails this time. On the first attempt, it shot passed the 158.75 mph (254 km/h) barrier. For the next attempt, the powder charge was increased. This time the charge was the

Yes, they are rockets (left)! Light them and the car will be propelled violently forward; unless it takes off, or even falls to pieces.

After a few attempts, von Opel thought it was preferable to run his "car" along rails (facing page). Wise decision.

equivalent of 825 lb. (375 kg) of dynamite, which the explosive experts were ordered to channel or "spin out" the explosion, i.e. make it progressive. They took an extra precaution, deciding to carry out a driverless test first. This was a good idea since the car exploded after three yards! The Imperial Railways Company pulled out of the project, but this wasn't enough to stop Fritz von Opel, who certainly had a nerve. He now wanted to test the rocket engine's results in air transport. A plane was got ready, by grafting on the usual battery of rockets, and getting the tail out of the path of the burning powder. This improbable machine was positioned on a sort of launching trolley, itself guided by fifty yards of tracks. Beyond that? Well, it'd be better if the plane had taken off by then. And it did take off. As though fired by a sling, the RAK-3 covered 2.5 miles (4 km) at more than an average of 93.75 mph (150 km). Then the rocket powder ran out and it had to land. Just a little detail: the machine didn't have any wheels. Its belly was simply fitted with a runner, enabling it to land in a "moderate fashion." Fritz ended this first recognized flight of a rocket plane by breaking a bit of wood, but he

rose to his feet and got out unhurt. The officials who ran up to help gave him a telegram from the Air Ministry forbidding the flight, but arriving strangely enough after takeoff.

After venting his energy in this way, Fritz von Opel could now return to the board meetings of the family firm whose corporate name he had so powerfully illuminated. This was some months before Opel was bought up by General Motors, a few months before the 1929 crash, a few short years before the great military turmoil which so destroyed Germany and which found other uses for Max Valier's rocket engine than distracting restless heirs.

Joel Woolf Barnato

1895-1948

A Wolf Out Hunting

Racing, okay, but as long as you win; every single time this dilettante driver took part in Le Mans he won. And to think that Woolf Barnato actually paid for the privilege to race!

Professional drivers today, tied to a manufacturer by a four-hundred-page legally validated contract, are paid footballers' salaries. They would find it hard to understand a chap like Woolf Barnato. The first difference, and it's a big one, was that Barnato did not have to wait for racing to make a fortune. Born in 1895, it happened that his father was the lucky owner of diamond mines, right at the other end of the British Empire, in South Africa. He was only very young when he lost his father, who committed suicide by throwing himself into the sea from the steamer taking him back to Great Britain. At the age of two, Woolf inherited several million pounds. Brought up in England, he cut the figure of a dandy, a young dilettante, a hedonist and aesthete, who roamed around the world for his pleasure; but his physique didn't really go with the role: he was suntanned, his hair was curly and rebellious, and he had impressive, broad shoulders earning him the scornful nickname "Babe." Babe boxed (in the heavyweight class), excelled at cricket and, of course, drove very fast.

In 1921, at the wheel of a huge Locomobile, he took part in several "occasional" competitions, just as one might knock a few balls about on a tennis court without actually being a listed, kitted-out, officially participating player, merely a member of the club. At Brooklands race track, he ran into other buffs, talked mechanics and driving,

races and records. Some of the chaps were really talented, others just full of hot air. Cars were swapped; there were races, challenges, and fun. Barnato's skills improved, as did his mechanical tastes. Soon he bought himself a Hispano-Suiza, then a Bentley; and it was through this that there was a decisive encounter, for Woolf and for Walter Owen Bentley, a self-taught engineer searching for quality at all costs. Very quickly becoming a privileged Bentley customer (he was so rich), Barnato had his Bentley endlessly improved; he won several races with it, which was excellent publicity for W. O. Bentley, who wanted even more. Would Barnato like to do something for the financial health of the company? In exchange, it became clear that Barnato would be part of the factory team, if that was what you could call the group, known as the "Bentley Boys," who were made up of a mix of honorary notables and mechanics who were paid yearly for other jobs apart from racing. Barnato contributed £100,000 to the cause, and as a result had at his disposal an excellent mount for winning the Le Mans 24 Hours race, which was quite something.

The 1928 race was one of the most keenly contested, but it came down to a duel between two rivals who overtook each other several times: the Stutz, driven by the Frenchmen Edouard Brisson and Robert Bloch, and the Bentley, driven by Barnato and Bernard Rubin. These four men shattered the

This "mechanic," who seems to have spent quite some time under his car, was actually one of the British Empire's wealthiest people (facing page).

distance records, despite the fog, the rain, and the still imperfect road surfaces. In the end, the Bentley won with less than a lap's lead.

The experience delighted Woolf Barnato: he was now a star driver and his influence within the firm doubled. He demanded continued technical innovations from the "boss," like fitting a compressor. In "civilian" life he liked cars as well. During a trip to the Riviera in 1930, he publicly challenged the famous "Blue Train" (Train Bleu) to a race. The Blue Train was legendary; it had sleeping cars with sumptuous cabins, varnished wood, prompt service; there were waxed mustaches, long dresses—a kind of Beau Brummell and Agatha Christie atmosphere. But Barnato won his bet easily, and stopped his Bentley in front of the very select St James's Club, in the heart of London, when the train had barely reached Calais. This original publicity for the brand, of which he was now the biggest shareholder and chairman, was not enough to revive sales, which

had been down since the Wall Street crash in 1929; to W. O. Bentley's despair, Barnato eventually abandoned the firm, leaving Rolls-Royce to swallow up its toughest rival.

Barnato retired from racing, sharing his time between his family and his business. He had two marriages and four children, one of whom—Mary—was to become one of the most famous English aviatrixes, qualified on Spitfires during the war and later the first English woman to break the sound barrier.

Woolf married a third time a few months before he died, in 1948. If proof were needed that he was still madly attached to the car he had helped develop, it could be found in the rather picturesque dispositions left for his funeral and discovered by his executors: the three-times winner of the Le Mans 24 Hours race, the brilliant Bentley Boy, was to be driven to his last resting place in one of those high period cars.

Brooklands, 1930: Barnato and Clement have just won the "Double Twelve," the twice-times 12 Hours race at Brooklands, in a Bentley Speed Six.

Brooklands, 1930 (left): despite attempts to stifle the engine noise a little (the famous "Brooklands Pipes," ending in a fishtail), the local residents finally got the track closed.

"Men will never stop being children; it's just the price of the toys that changes." This was particularly true of Barnato who, in order to obtain a better car, bought into Bentley (below).

André Derain
1880-1954

Traveling in Color

It was a question of considering the car as a new object
to be seen but, above all, as a new point of view.
Derain, the inventor-painter, found his inspiration in Bugattis.

André Derain painted his first pictures near Chatou, where he was born in 1880. He was just fifteen and already ahead of the crowd. He was a copyist at the Louvre and practiced copying Flemish art. It was the last period of calm before the storm that the twentieth century blew across art. Painting dates back to the cave pictures of Lascaux, whereas the car had just been invented. Some artists up there in their studios didn't even see it going past. Others were thoroughly upset by it. Earlier, there had been J. M. W. Turner who tried to grasp the magic of a train moving. Filippo Tommaso Marinetti, in his "Futurist Manifesto," proclaimed in 1909 that "a roaring motor car which seems to run on machine-gun fire, is more beautiful than the Victory of Samothrace,"[1] and called on painting to convey our "tumultuous life of steel, pride, fever and speed." Following him was a cohort of gladiators, paintbrushes at the ready, pointing forward, trying to capture speed on canvas. And some of them even succeeded— Umberto Boccioni, for instance.

André Derain didn't need to be convinced by futurist theories. He liked driving as much as painting. But he denied ever being an intellectual; he had left school for a mechanics class and then that for the Académie, where he joined those least academic of masters, Henri Matisse and Maurice de Vlaminck. Austere painting, methodical workshops, and wise discussions were not for him. But what about travel—Collioure first, then London—what about boldness, what about colors? Derain dared

everything and succeeded in everything. When a critic qualified him as a "fauve", (wild beast) —coining this new art movement— it was no doubt refering as much to his rebellious manners as to the vivid tones of his paint palette.

Derain visited, took in, understood, directed, and stimulated other artists. His women *Bathers* formed a link between Cézanne, who influenced them, and Picasso, whom they influenced. This was just before *Les Demoiselles d'Avignon*. With the ebullience and the disruption of traditions and ideas, the painters of the time were students who respected nothing, and philosophers who scrutinized the passing of a picture, from the real to the idea, like atomic scientists with light, or neurologists with our retinas. On his journey through life, and without making any concessions, André Derain became famous, which made him more money than his father's creamery had done. It was at the wheel of his Bugatti that Man Ray immortalized him; it was an expensive car, an almost unique car, an artist's object. And Derain knew Rembrandt Bugatti, the animal sculptor, the brother of the carmaker and a delicate artist, who committed suicide in 1916, after his return from the front where he had been serving as a volunteer stretcher-bearer.

The dangers of excessive emotion were there indeed: of course, a number of "modern" painters hacked along, grasped at certain effortless effects to get out of hours of studying, and rushed towards the same prestige acquired by the authentic researchers, earned as a result

Painting: an ordinary pastime or a means of seizing reality? The car: a vulgar time-saver or a knife for cutting into the countryside? Derain (facing page) loved both.

of their long vigils. Of *Les Demoiselles d'Avignon*, Derain said: "One day we shall find Pablo has hanged himself behind his great canvas." It gives an idea of the suffering, of the true effort made in this authentic pursuit of truth beyond realism.

The Bugatti attracted the artist's sensitivity, by the elegance of its lines and its fussy finish, its love of form even where the mechanical parts were concerned. But this was not the essential thing. In Derain's hands, a really fast car was also an instrument of perception, showing us how the countryside, when we plunge into it, deforms itself and distends itself. With the tip of your right foot, you change the composition and even the density of the countryside you're going through, which in itself is upset, fragmented, up to the pointillism that Derain foresaw at Collioure.

Later on in life, Derain was like a disenchanted star, burning all he had adored. But what about fauvism? "It's for the cleaners," he said. He did without almost any color when he painted his last series of paintings, the *Paysages Tristes* ("Melancholy Lanscapes") and the *Sinistres* ("Disasters"). But right until the end he loved his Bugattis and other high-powered cars, and what they got him to see. He was killed in a car accident in 1954. Was he looking elsewhere?

1. Translation taken from James Joll, *Three Intellectuals in Politics*, Pantheon Books, 1961.

Road, 1932: did Derain capture this road heading off into the setting sun through a windshield (above left)?

A good number of painters traveled to the Midi for the light. Derain (above) stayed in Monaco, where no doubt he seized the chance to watch the Grand Prix.

Derain and his Bugatti
35A, which was closely
related to the racing
machines (above).
One of the best
automobiles you could
buy for taking bends.

Jean Bugatti
1909-1939

A Young Man of Means

A nice-looking young man, wearing a light suit, and a hat over his eyes—in the Paris of the Thirties, both the real artist's bohemia and the fashionable dandy's bohemia scrutinized Jean Bugatti. He was a young industrialist, the heir to a luxury brand-name, a skilled racing driver, and an elegant artist.

Very impressive; and, to add to all that, when Jean Bugatti screeched off at the wheel of an exceptional car, it was often one that he himself had designed.

He was a young man of means. When discussing the Bugattis, you first have to talk about the grandfather, Carlo. He was a cabinetmaker who created unique objects, according to art nouveau aesthetics: a bed frame, for example, made of scrolls, with supple plant shapes containing the bed side at the end of one "branch," and the other cut out into a canopy.

Carlo christened his sons, born like him in the Milan area, Ettore and Rembrandt. The younger went on to be a great sculptor, only just escaping the destiny that his first name might have decreed. The elder became a driver, mechanic, engineer, inventor, and finally an industrialist, but he was like an artist too. He could design a car from the tip of the headlights to the tip of the brakes, and sold the De Dietrich company a complete prototype in 1900. He was nineteen. Then he worked for Mathis and for Deutz in Cologne where his son, Jean, was born. For Peugeot, he designed the Bébé, a little jewel of visionary simplification, one of the first popular cars. And then, in 1910, Ettore settled in the Alsatian (German) town of Molsheim. There he founded, in his own name, what was to become the most famous car company of the prewar period.

As master in his own house, Ettore organized his stables (his first hobby was keeping thoroughbreds) and set the highest manufacturing standards ever, without at all worrying about what his rivals could put into the field against him. Between 1910 and 1939, Bugatti produced and sold 7,500 cars. In the same period, Renault, for instance, shifted 885,000. This was not the same market, or the same price. With a Bugatti, each mechanical part was meticulously crafted, both technically and aesthetically. With lathes they made themselves, the craftsmen machined parts whose finish still fills people with wonder. The customers quickly took charge of promoting Molsheim. No other make won so many races: thirty-eight Grand Prix and three thousand victories by various sporting customers.

Prosperity came with this reputation and Bugatti was at the apogee of his career. His tall silhouette was magnified by a lordly portliness. Ettore reigned. On his overalls there was an embroidered name: "The Boss." Like a sovereign monarch, surrounded by his family and his court of clients, he carried on with his superb, hare-brained ideas, piled up inspired patents and zany inventions, went around the circuits in an

"The Boss's son": Jean Bugatti was a dandy (facing page), as at ease in society as he was on the shop floor at Molsheim.

extraordinary, ultramodern trailer, and had his saddlers make him "foot gloves." He christened his second daughter Ebé, after his own initials, which were also the make's logo.

He stifled his son, too, with his arrogance; he hadn't expected to see Jean as his successor so soon. Jean was self-taught, but at the best school: the workers gradually taught him all they knew; they were the best there was. When Jean was not in the factory, he was at Gangloff's, a little coachworks in Colmar, which had expanded because it did Bugatti's bodywork. Seeing the chassis start off with nothing on it filled him with enthusiasm; seeing the bodywork being built filled him with wonder; seeing the whole thing being put together to become a complete car really gripped him.

Watching the show from the wings can either make an artist's soul cynical or enthuse it and give it the means to create earlier. The latter was the case. Jean sketched his first bodywork design when he was very young, and his ideas were at the heart of some of the most beautiful and boldest Bugattis.

On the technical side, his father had been a great innovator when he'd started, and although he believed in the solutions he had worked out, he had now become the most conservative of industrialists. The Bugattis were gradually being caught up by other less swanky, more pragmatic makes. Jean thought up some innovations and prolongations which both spared his father's susceptibilities and met the demands of the times.

Whereas Ettore designed the Royale, a car with a capital "C," a real giant, which was worth the price of three Rolls-Royces, Jean improved the Type 57. He designed a modern front suspension with independent wheels, and tested it himself using an unspecified car

whose emblematic horseshoe radiator had been replaced by an ordinary sloping radiator grill. In order to be able to talk to the technicians about this prototype, which his father didn't even know existed, they had agreed on a code: "crème de menthe." At this time, and under his covert orders, the Bugattis were dominant again and triumphed at Le Mans in 1937 and 1939.

Jean the reformer was held back by a father who, ever since the social conflict in Alsace in 1936, together with accumulating financial difficulties, seemed to show less interest in his factory than in his horses and in his second family in Paris. Even so, he didn't allow his son any more leeway. As for Jean's third talent, driving racing cars, Ettore categorically refused to allow it.

In June 1939, a Bugatti 57 with revolutionary styling designed by Jean, once again beat all its rivals at the Le Mans 24 Hours race. The following 11 August, on his way back from Sarthe, on the pretext that tests needed to be carried out, and no doubt also hoping to improve it, Jean took the car out near the factory and his home. Two mechanics closed the entrance, letting only a cyclist through. What happened? Was it to avoid him? The fact remains that a swerve at full speed was fatal for the beautiful blue car, for Jean Bugatti, and probably for the prestige of the French automobile industry. Less than a month later, war broke out. The Reich annexed Alsace while Ettore, the Italian refugee in Paris, refused any invitation to carry on producing. The fabulous factory at Molsheim was given to the engineer and former stormtrooper, Hans Trippel, who made amphibious vehicles for the Wehrmacht.

Ettore died in 1947. His firm trundled along under Roland, the last son. There were a number of attempts to rekindle the firm but they lacked Jean's light elegance and enlightened dandyism.

Jean Bugatti, like his cabinet-maker father, his sculptor uncle and his engineer father, blended technique with aesthetics.
The roof was made in two parts, welded into a crest which became a decorative element (facing page top).

The Bugatti 57C, winner at Le Mans with Wimille (hairband) and Veyron (facing page bottom). It owed its eight-cylinder twin-cam engine and its profiling to Jean.
Two months later he killed himself trying it out in front of his father's factory.

A Type 43 with roadster bodywork by Jean Bugatti (top). The long curve on the front wing was his signature.

The impressive prow of a Type 57. The thin wheels were faired as closely as possible (center).

Beneath the dust from the race, the car can appear to be rustic and badly finished. But today, restored with care, this 57 from the 1937 Le Mans shows the care and finish given to every detail (bottom).

Jean's golfing trousers date the photograph almost as well as the high horseshoe radiator grill (facing page).

13 Rue Forey - Paris   S. Henry

Hellé Nice

1900-1984

Naked Speed

Hellé Nice's job was frivolity. She danced nude, which was the type of job that rather stamps the story of your life forever. So what is the connection between a music-hall stage where you dance and whirl around in front of theater stalls full of lecherous men, and a bend taken at great speed watched by thousands of spectators?

What do a beautiful showgirl from the Casino de Paris and a racing driver have in common? Is it the public, newspapers, flowers, money, stage fright? Neither activity is commonplace. Of course, there's the risk of making a fool of yourself, but there's also the opportunity to please people.

One of the Casino de Paris's star dancers, "Hellé Nice" went on tour all round Europe. At twenty-six, she owned a house and a boat. Not bad for someone born Hélène Delangle, the daughter of the postman at Aunay-sous-Auneau, a tiny village in northern France. She went up to Paris at sixteen, right in the middle of the war, and began moving in the most enjoyable, trendy circles, among people who lounged around and were prepared to finance the most agreeable escapades and the most assertive talents generously.

Hellé Nice also skied, remarkably well, too. In 1929 she entered her Omega in Montlhéry, the women's Grand Prix. She won and beat a speed record on the way, traveling at an average of 123.75 mph (198 km/h). The circuit, although rather imposing, did not impress her. And she liked the character she was playing. The gossips might say she was running after men, but she would be a racing driver. One of those with a good record,

like Jean Bugatti, Philippe de Rothschild, and so on. She met Rothschild when she came back from the States, where she had been to dance and drive a Miller in dirt-track races, skidding around in the dust. Rothschild introduced her to Bugatti, who entrusted her with a 35C, which she immediately had painted a very recognizable light blue and at the wheel of which she lined up for "men's" Grand Prix. Starting bonuses and publicity contracts replaced the music-hall engagements, but it was still the same job, the same nerve. Like the sequins and the dancer's tutu (or rather lack of tutu), the rough canvas overalls, and leather hairband were clothes that had to be worn for all to see. What was left was originality, charm, a certain solitude; in short, refinement.

When you're pretty, some people can't imagine you have any real depth. People can't conceive that there's any real talent hiding behind a coquettish appearance. Colette, the writer, suffered from the same narrow-mindedness before Héllé Nice. But such a woman might be more accurately typecast, (although typecasting can never be an accurate reflection of the truth), as a libertine and a liberated woman.

It may seem that driving was more for show, a sort of pleasant diversion, the sort of activity that

Like Colette, Hellé Nice worked in music hall (facing page). Like "La Garçonne," Victor Margueritte's heroine, she loved cars; a woman who behaved so badly but who drove so well: quite a disconcerting mix.

Free and proud of it? Even just before the start of a race, Hellé Nice remembers to "model" her elegant racing suit (left and below). This was at a time when for a woman to wear trousers was scandalous.

Hellé Nice spent most of her career driving Bugattis, but it was with an Alfa Romeo 8C (left) that she achieved her best results.

makes the gentlemen's eyes twinkle, but also gets them worried about in what way they are actually supposed to be better than women. It was the sort of activity that disconcerted the elegant women yawning on the side of the tracks, finding racing cars much too rustic, and frightened of snagging their beautiful flowery dresses on simple bolts; and then there were all those greasy, oily stains, and those terrible smells. But that would be to forget that, although the theater can harm a reputation, the track can break bodies. Her stable mates, famous drivers, often fell in the races. Hellé Nice got caught up in it all. Being continuously audacious, coupled with the experience of seventy-five Grand Prix, made her into a devilishly fast driver.

Her destiny coincided with certain milestones: 1936 was the end of the Roaring Twenties in France and the beginning of another epoch. At that time, Hellé Nice was in South America for a season of races aboard an Alfa Romeo 8C—what a machine! It was more powerful, even faster than a Bugatti, and just as red as the other was blue. In the São Paulo Grand Prix she was second and catching up with the Brazilian champion, Manuel de Teffé. There was a problem. Was it caused by another driver's clumsiness? Was it a spectator wanting to protect "his" driver? Suddenly, there was a bale of straw in front of the Alfa Romeo's wheels as it came out of a bend. The car smashed into it, left the track and flew into the stands where it spread death and destruction. Thrown out of her seat, Nice was seriously injured; she was thought to be dead.

The Brazilian newspapers made the most of the drama, telling how she had been thrown onto a young soldier who died as a result. Nice woke up out of a coma after three days. Brazil was fascinated by the story: "Elenice" became a first name there.

In 1937, Nice was back behind the wheel again: it was her only job. But she'd lost her nerve. She returned to Montlhéry to set an impressive series of female world endurance records: taking turns with four other women, she drove a Matford V8 for ten days and ten nights over 20,000 miles (32,000 km).

Hellé eschewed the tracks for a while, during upheavals in her life and those caused by the war. In 1949 a big ball was organized for the start of the Monte Carlo rally, which she signed up for. Louis Chiron, the Monegasque driver and the rally's influential manager, accused her publicly of having been a Gestapo agent. It was the end of her career.

Was the accusation founded? No biographer, for or against her, has ever found the slightest proof of any involvement with the Gestapo. Nevertheless, Hellé had lost her reputation, her means of existence, the lifestyle she enjoyed.

Much later, aged more than sixty, she drove the Simca Trianon belonging to the "La Roue Tourne" Foundation, which helps destitute artists. It was a sort of epilog that brought her two jobs together and suggested that the racing driver's job was also part of the art of show business. And why not?

Tazio Nuvolari

1892-1953

Bullfighter

Champion, eternal champion: why did Nuvolari deserve this status?
It was probably because he thought racing was more important
than everything else, which isn't the case for all racing drivers,
but may be more common among the better bullfighters.

Tazio Nuvolari was an Italian, but one of the best races at the beginning of his career took place in Spain, where the local press called him the "Conductor del Emociòn" ("The Emotion Driver"). Their comparing him to a matador was no exaggeration. He had the same elegance in the arena, the same boldness in the face of danger, the same resistance to unhappiness and pain, the same vain affectation, the same sense of show. Racing was everything.

Ferdinand Porsche, who had seen him racing when he was an engineer with Auto Union, described him publicly as the "best racing driver of the past, present and future." Many sports historians still have the same opinion. Why did Tazio make people dream more than any other driver?

His tally was indeed impressive: two Targa Florios, two Mille Miglias, the only Le Mans 24 Hours in which he took part, and ten international Grand Prix, the equivalents of the present-day Formula 1, which he won on the most beautiful circuits: the Nürburgring, Rheims, Monza, Monaco, etc.

But others did just as well. So how do you explain that special aura surrounding Nuvolari? Was it his magnetism, his character?

Perhaps the Nuvolari legend had something to do with his atypical career. When at last he was able to take part in competitions, he was twenty-eight, the age at which our childhood champions tend to start thinking about converting to publicity, for instance. He started with motorbikes, which is when his legendary status began too. The races were often organized by the local authorities; often took place in the street themselves. He stuffed his racing suit so that he could push himself off the house walls with his elbows and thereby get through faster! During the 1925 Grand Prix des Nations, he fell and broke his hand, got up again and won, the bones sticking out of the torn glove. The public immediately took to this little man with the long face, who put everything into winning. He had the same incredible commitment when he moved onto driving cars. During one of the Italian Grand Prix in 1925, he drove an enormous Bianchi, whose tires burst one after the other, but he won and finished on the wheel rims, with sparks flying and metal screeching. Neubauer, the boss at Mercedes and therefore one of his rivals, spoke of his dark and almost "demoniacal character."

His devilish way of driving was not just a matter of risk taking. Nuvolari was a great driving technician who liked to be provocative, saying that "brakes were no use." Even his peers were intrigued by his talent. Enzo Ferrari, who was not actually renowned for his compliments, recalled how, impressed by his stable-mate's times, he clambered aboard with him for a trial. The great Mr. Ferrari, who knew a thing or two about driving, recalls in his memoirs, *My Terrible Joys*, that when

Small, with a long face, Tazio Nuvolari shared the appeal of the cars he mastered and dominated (facing page); he tamed their violent natures.

they came into sight of the first bend, he was sure they would never get round it. Nuvolari was taking it much too fast! Then, as if by miracle, from a skid triggered with determination and accuracy and in a class of its own, the driver put the wheels of the Alfa Romeo round the bend. And so it was with each bend. For the spectators, any driver who could "out-drive" each portion of the road like that became an unforgettable hero. Today, the width of the tires and the precision of the electronic devices mean that this way of driving is condemned as being too slow. But maybe, if Nuvolari were still alive. . . .

In order to have a better career, he needed a worthy rival, an alter ego, a favorite enemy. Nuvolari's turned out to be Achille Varzi. All Italy was divided, as with football, in their support of one or other of these two drivers, who were completely opposite. Varzi was charming, a good speaker, very elegant, easily ironical. Alfred Neubauer said: "Even when Varzi climbed into his car, the pleat on his overall trousers was impeccable. Nuvolari's were always creased and his sleeves rolled up."

Tazio climbed aboard his car wearing rather casual gear, but he also stubbornly wore a yellow pullover with the picture of a tortoise drawn by Gabriele d'Annunzio. At a time when the upper part of the driver's body was visible above the car sides. he could be recognized among all the others wearing this outfit. In the 1930 Mille Miglia, a 1,000 mile (1,600-km), uninterrupted road race starting and finishing in Brescia, Nuvolari finished with an average of more than 62.5 mph (100 km/h). In order to catch up with Varzi by surprise, legend has it that Nuvolari who had left after him, drove for a long time without headlights by moonlight. Spare a thought for Guidotti, the co-driver during this "exploit."

Where did Tazio Nuvolari come from? His father and a brother were champion cyclists; his grandfather was one of Garibaldi's companions and a prominent member of his supporters, the Redshirts. He had no money, but a certainty that he was talented gave him determination enough to line up for as many competitions as possible. So that he could race, he set up his own stable, in the same way an acrobat with no trapeze would create a whole circus to feed his family; for that was his ultimate aim. Mad about driving though he was, Nuvolari was a pious and orderly family man, providing a house for his family, then ensuring his sons received a good education. Little by little his reputation got him more competitive engagements.

He used all sorts of cars: Alfa Romeos, Bugattis, MGs Auto Unions, Ferraris, and so on. He often defeated the leading machines driving an outmoded car, which he alone knew how to supercharge. Thus he was the only one in the 1935 season to beat the German machines, with an Alfa P3, which was 30 percent less powerful, and, what was more, he beat them in the German Grand Prix. At the end of the race that Hitler had attended to salute his machines' triumph, the organizers of the Nürburgring hadn't even got a recording of the Italian national anthem. But that didn't matter; Nuvolari had one in his luggage!

A virtuoso with front-engined cars, Nuvolari dared to challenge the "P Wagen," Auto Union's central-engined cars by Dr Porsche. Even though his Alfa P3 was significantly less powerful (above), he still managed to win the German Grand Prix.

Tazio's Alfa Romeo
sports the Cavallino,
the badge of the
Scuderia, the Ferrari
team (above).
An unforgettable
union of talents.

This affront was the surest way of getting a car with Auto Union (the ancestor of Audi).

So in 1938, the four-ringed firm which had just lost its number one driver, Bernd Rosemeyer, in a record-breaking attempt, took on Nuvolari. This was at the pinnacle of the domination of the Silver Arrows—the German machines from Mercedes and Auto Union—and the rivalry between the two German teams was at its height. As they were built with racing funds offered by the Reich, the cars all carried a black swastika on their sides. Although he was used to all sorts of machines and all sorts of competitions, he hadn't yet driven a car with a centrally mounted engine, for the very good reason that this layout, designed by Dr. Porsche, was exclusive to Auto Union. Although talent, vision, and speed sensations were the same, all the driving movements were different compared to a traditional car with a front-mounted engine and rear-wheel drive, not to mention the power, 500 bhp, which he hadn't yet encountered.

Few champions would be able, at the age of forty-six, to start their apprenticeship all over again and have to rethink the whole of their own technique. But "Nivola," as the Italian admirers called him, became one of the best Auto Union specialists, and he only needed a few races to outdo Mercedes and the proven champions like Rudi Caracciola, Hermann Lang or the young Dick Seaman, Mercedes' young hope who perished tragically the same year. At aged more than forty-six, Nuvolari won three major victories: the 1938 Great Britain and Italy Grand Prix and the 1939 Yugoslav Grand Prix on September 3, the day the war started.

For a champion to be truly honored—God knows why—there must also perhaps be something vulnerable about him. Tazio's numerous injuries, followed every time by a thunderous return to the tracks, were doubtless not enough, even if tragedy dogged him. After the war and the postwar period, which probably robbed him of ten years' successes, Nuvolari made a comeback. He was destroyed physically, for what we now know as tuberculosis was eating up his lungs. During a race he would often lift himself higher than the edge of the windscreen to force air into his ailing lungs. His morale was destroyed too. The death of his two sons, one after the other, and from the same disease, had removed his reason for living. But his driving was intact. Unhappiness and illness, which so often get you down, proved to be sources of renewed strength for driving and racing for him. Speed was his talent, his ally, his refuge, and his consolation. In 1948 he was a hair's breadth (or rather a strand in the steel of his Ferrari's crankshaft) from winning the Mille Miglia, the great classic of those days, for the third time. From then on he ended each race on the verge of passing out, though he never announced he was retiring.

Tazio Nuvolari died on August 11, 1953 at Padua. His funeral was attended by some twenty-five thousand people.

Much later, the memory of the flying Mantuan was honored by two prototypes, two of those dream cars on which manufacturers confer all their designers' reputation for the duration of a single car show: two of them! The Alfa Romeo Nuvola (1996) and the Audi Nuvolari (2003). Perhaps Nivola, despite all his keenness and his pride, would not have imagined the shadow of his exploits being cast so far forward in time.

At the wheel of a Bugatti 35 during the Monaco Grand Prix (facing page top), he took part several times—and won in 1932—but with an Alfa.

Alfred Neubauer
1891–1980

Don Alfredo

His corpulent silhouette with his hat, braces, and shapeless raincoat, could often be seen on the side of the track. Which track?
Well, almost all the European and American ones, from the sunny, dusty roads of the Targa Floria to the windy motorways of the developing Germany of the Thirties.

In 1900 or just before, a car passing through a small village of northern Moravia, in what is now the Czech Republic, covered the main street with dust. It was a Benz; little Alfred watched it go by, and gazed for a long time at the point where it had disappeared. The feeling he had at that moment is what is known as a sense of vocation. Immediately he started collecting all the catalogs from the carmakers, gulping down any information that in one way or another could bring him nearer to driving. At twenty-three, nothing had yet happened. Then the 1914 war broke out, and he realized that knowing something about mechanics might be a way to avoid the trenches. A few twists of fate later, and still the same vocation, and Neubauer found himself with Austro-Daimler, under Dr. Porsche, the busy engineer who often changed companies, but rarely ideas. Porsche appreciated Neubauer for his organizing skills and took him with him to Mercedes.

For the young Alfred, the focal point of his vocation was still a racing car's steering wheel. "I was convinced that glory and fortune were there for the taking if I could become a driver." In his memoirs,[1] he was fairly harsh about his own illusions. He described himself as a clumsy, pretentious person, gazing bitterly at a race track from a neighboring field into which he had inopportunely crashed

his car, watched mockingly by a beginner called Rudi Caracciola. Another picaresque episode took place at the Semmering hill-climb races. As the first of a stable of four Daimlers, he reached the summit, very pleased with a performance he almost considered unbeatable. The times set by his three colleagues struck three blows, one after the other, at his enthusiasm. His own reaction was typical of any driver: he suspected that "something had gone wrong with the timekeeping," but it was his girlfriend who dealt the final blow. "The other three drive like madmen but you, you drive like a night-watchman." Though his taste for racing and speed remained unchanged, this revelation was certainly pretty painful. On the other hand, Neubauer practically invented the job of team manager.

This was during the Thirties. At the time drivers were treated like princes. The show they provided and the risks they took earned them immense popular prestige, worthy of entertainers. Neubauer acted as a go-between. He represented the manufacturers' interests with the drivers, and the drivers' with the manufacturers. It was a curious position to be in life, managing, and imposing your will and discipline on all those young people who took the worst risks imaginable, many of whom would

Alfred Neubauer (facing page) was a driver for a time and could never be very far from a racing car. He achieved fame and success running the Mercedes stable during its most successful years.

die. He was also the intercessor between life and tragedy. It was he who had to look at the technical reasons behind an accident, which certainly did not mean that he wasn't affected by the tragic dimension when one of his lads disappeared. When Auto Union, the rival company, lost Bernd Rosemeyer in a record-breaking attempt, Neubauer insisted on trying to determine what exactly had occurred on this section of German highway when the car had crashed at more than 280 mph (450 km/h). He eventually found the trace of a gusting crosswind in the anemometric readings from a weather station coincided with the precise moment that Rosemeyer had passed through a clearing.

Neubauer knew that when the racing driver is doing his job, he is "one of the loneliest people in the world." Thanks to his organizing skills, he was able to deal with communication problems between the drivers and the pits. In 1926, on the Solitudering at Stuttgart, he introduced a system of signs—panels and flags—which changed racing history. From then on it was possible to transmit pieces of information but also orders: it was the beginning of team discipline.

But if he'd been thinking about all that, it was also so he could reduce his own anxiety. Imagine, with the dangers from the weather, what state of mind the boss would be in when he saws "his" cars going past on the Nürburgring and going out of sight for a whole lap, almost ten minutes! At least he could carry on doing things, timing, preparing the signs for the next pass. The "dictator" suffered. As on that day there was a heatwave, on the Avus circuit where, as he recalls: "I was a bundle of nerves. The suffering and the agony of the tires in such weather were terrifying."

Rivals sometimes disappeared; sometimes it was his own men, like the young hopeful Dick Seaman, whom Neubauer himself had unearthed. These losses moved him enormously and affected him; but he was inflexible: it didn't stop him sending his drivers back onto the track. He remained on the edge of the tracks, "his mouth dry with emotion."

But racing wasn't just about tragedies, and it was in race-track routine that Neubauer showed how good he was. Always trying to be better organized meant you kept bad luck at bay. He inaugurated the systematic tire-changing training sessions, improved the refueling conditions, and managed the Mille Miglia logistics, a race that was so difficult for foreign makes.

The 1930s Silver Arrow Mercedes raced as much for the prestige of the Reich (which financed the company) as they did for the brand with the three-branched star; car racing was elevated to the dangerous role of manifesto for the New Order. How did the "fat man," whose

Neubauer adored driving and, like all drivers, thought he was the best. But at the wheel of Mercedes SSs (left) and SKs, he realized that his stable-mates were much better than he was.

A formidable organizer, Neubauer also enjoyed having fun (left). He is pretending to put Stirling Moss under starter's orders as he leaves the factory at the wheel of his company 280 SL.

authority, even when it was visionary, was based on competence, put up with the SS officer with whom the authorities had saddled him as a financial controller—or was it as confessor or political commissary? He bided his time, protected as best he could Hans Stuck, who was both idealized as the Aryan champion and persecuted because it was discovered that his wife's grandmother was Jewish.

Neubauer also became an improvised coach on occasions. He put together a "special cocktail" for the driver in which you could find—among other things—Malaga, black coffee, sugar, egg yolk, and various spices. He was also known for his temper. He was banned from Irish race tracks after exploding with rage and calling the officials "pigs" and shouting other obscenities—he alas spoke several languages—after what he thought was an unjustified disqualification.

Alfred Neubauer, nicknamed the "Fat Man," or "Don Alfredo," was both demanding to the point of hardness and undeniably affectionate with some of his drivers; he was perpetually at loggerheads with organizers and rule-writers of all kinds; he had an unbending love of racing. He successively raced Hermann Lang, Manfred von Brauchitsch, Rudi Caracciola, then Stirling Moss, Juan Manuel Fangio, etc.

The drivers who got close to him knew his real personality. In his foreword to Neubauer's

autobiography, Stirling Moss spoke of "an amazing character, who could have anybody snapping to attention if necessary, but would also show great thought and understanding, in relaxed moments he could have us all rolling about with laughter." [2] For Stirling Moss, he became a stable manager because he loved racing cars but he would have succeeded in any other career or business and even on stage, had he so desired.

This authoritarian manager did indeed have the knack of imitating people, with a repertoire ranging from Adolf Hitler to Marilyn Monroe. But above all he knew how to read his drivers' thoughts, both at work and outside. Well before there was any telemetry or any television, he knew how to tell "when a driver had had a problem with a bend," or if on the other hand he had been let down by his tires, or by something the mechanics had done, or had been pushed off the track by a rival.

Neubauer only left the racing world when Mercedes withdrew for the last time, in 1955, and then looked after the firm's Stuttgart museum. It was in 1980 that he joined all those young men who, as he had written earlier, "one day climbed into their silvery machines and left for an unknown destination, where we all go sooner or later."

1. *Speed Was My Life,* translated and edited by Stewart Thomson and Charles Meisl, Barrie and Rockliff, 1960.
2. Ibid.

Blaise Cendrars
1887-1961

The One-armed Virtuoso

Blaise Cendrars, the Swiss novelist and poet, seemed to live a life of endless turmoil. In 1915, he lost his right arm while serving with the French Foreign Legion, but that did not stop him from driving cars—of all sorts—and always very fast.

A car aficionado, Cendrars? Well yes, that and the rest. He was a scriptwriter in Hollywood, a publicist in Paris, a juggler in London. He was also an infantryman on the Marne in 1914, (he joined the French Foreign Legion because he was Swiss), an extra for Abel Gance, (then assistant on the film *La Roue*), and then went on to become a painter like his friends Marc Chagall and Fernand Léger. And he never stopped traveling: from Moscow in 1905 to Brazil in the Twenties, via London as a young man, Naples as a child, and Arles as a recluse during World War II. And, of course, he was a writer too. He was a novelist, and a keen scribbler, as well as a special correspondent and journalist for "real" newspapers and for himself. But when you're a "real" journalist, all life is reporting. And, last but not least, he was a poet; Cendrars was always a poet.

"All of life is nothing but a poem, a movement."[1] He was a complete writer, keen and untidy, bulimic and sporadic; he was a writer right up to his adopted name, Blaise Cendrars, which was a mix of "*braise*" and "*cendres*" (ember and ashes); his real name was Frédéric Sauser. For him "writing was to be burnt alive, but also to rise from one's ashes."

He'd already had a car accident—on the Saint-Cloud Hill near Paris—in 1913 in which he'd broken a leg. Nothing more was ever known about the accident. Was it the kind of accident that's typical of a youngster; was he even driving? Or was he a passenger in one of these dramatic moments of life he seemed to always be experiencing?

Traveling to Brazil, to the Arctic, California, the Kremlin, or becalmed in a minute port, at La Redonne, protected from the tourists by a very steep hill that you could only get a car up if it were hauled up by a team: "I owed my popularity and my adoption by the eight fishermen to my car. They complimented me on it, the way it so easily tore me away, lifted me up, and climbed the fateful hill without any hesitation. 'That's an engine!' they said, 'just like a plane.' I'd say! That Sunbeam developed almost 200 bhp."[2]

Sometimes he acted as host to the American novelist and artist John Dos Passos when he and his wife, Katy, were traveling down to Spain. The latter wrote: "We'd cook wild geese in a huge chimney and we ate truffle omelets every day. Afterwards, we'd leave in the car along the little mountain roads. It was a terrifying experience. He drove with one hand, changing gears, God knows how. He took all the bends at his usual top speed. God only knows how we survived."

And it certainly wasn't simple to drive cars then. The gearbox was as big as an engine and had itself to be driven, accompanied, and caressed: there was no synchronization. You had to declutch, push the lever into neutral, release

A man of ceaseless energy, Cendrars was a doer as well as an observer; contemplative yet restless (facing page). He regarded cars (and trains and boats as well) as a means of experiencing life more intensely.

the clutch and with the same movement let the engine go again to launch the transmission gearwheel. When that maneuver is well done, the gear lever is drawn from the palm of your hand, without any screeching; the engine brake is already helping the wheel brakes and the gear has been changed, ready for the acceleration that alone can guide you round the bend. All that was like a ballet, but the time needed to change gears was effectively "free" time for the steering wheel to spin where it wanted to; especially when you're like Blaise Cendrars and you've lost your right arm. But he knew the trajectory intuitively, poetically. He drove as he wrote.

Despite the periods of poverty that Cendrars endured, he still managed to drive fine cars, including an Alfa Romeo 6C 1750, one of the very first real sports cars, very low slung, fine, pared down, both rustic and refined, and hellishly expensive—though it was an old car, it was true, for by now it was 1940 and Cendrars was a war correspondent at the Arras HQ, stationed behind the lines during the fall of France.

Moving around again, as he always had, Cendrars traveled by boat and train, too; but the author of *La Prose du Transsibérien* ("Prose of the Trans-Siberian"), 1913, always had a car lurking in the pages of his books. They were chosen accessories, characters in their own right, or instruments used for making life more intense. "At the wheel, I'm aiming at the heart of loneliness; I sit in the delight of contemplation with my foot on the accelerator. My thoughts fly. I have no regrets, no more desires." [2]

His novels chronicle his life, as in this passage from *L'Homme foudroyé* (*The Astonished Man*), originally published in 1945.

"What am I going to do in Paris?

"The Traction had arrived; it's a very low slung machine, exceptionally light with front wheel drive, and it can reach 180.

"It's powerful and supple; its pulling power and its keenness to split the air give you the impression you're flying. You can't forget that impression once you've encountered it. And the way it takes bends is like a dream. This is no

In the Thirties, Cendrars got his hands on this Alfa 6C (above) which he always drove flat out.

Polygraphic Cendrars (facing page): producing scenarios, reports, tales, novels. A compulsive writer, this was another outlet for the energy that flowed so strongly through him.

car, it's a plane. The 'plane of the road', said the mechanic who'd brought it from Paris for me.

"Good, good.

"I gave the chap the wherewithal to go home by train, by a special train if he wanted and I settled aboard the car, alone.

"He looked so miserable, annoyed at being left there, so much so that I gave him my best smile. My last smile.

"I grabbed the wheel, I pressed the starter, I let in the clutch and I thundered off. I was going to try my luck again.

"If only I could drive off the road and crash!"[3]

In fact his story's ending was less violent; in 1960 he was given the title of Commander of the Légion d'honneur for his service in wartime, and he died the following year.

1. Extract from an article written by Cendrars and published in *Der Sturm,* 1913.
2. Sonia Delaunay and Blaise Cendrars, *La Prose du Transsibérien et de la petite Jehanne de France,* Editions des Hommes Nouveaux, 1913. (Our translation)
3. *L'Homme foudroyé,* Denoël, 1945. (Our translation)

Robert Benoist

1895–1944

The Elegance of Being Untamable

Courage is often cited as being one of the many qualities a racing driver needs. But there are several types of courage. There is physical courage, when you have to face the terrible sensations of speed at the controls of a Spad fighter or a Delage Torpedo. But there is also the kind of courage you need to carry on when racing has killed a friend.

There is stubbornness in the face of life's vicissitudes, and the courage to oppose an unjust occupation: to resist torture and refuse to talk. Robert Benoist possessed all types.

He was born on Saint Benoît's Day at Saint-Benoît in northern France. His parents were stewards on the Rothschild property, set amid woodland, where a taste for hunting could be indulged, shooting and stalking skills learned—a premonition of those required by resistance fighters. But young Robert's fascination lay in mechanics, and he decided on an apprenticeship in a Versailles garage. He chose racing also, on a bike first. As a young man of his times, he was a mechanic with Grégoire at Poissy, with Unic at Puteaux; then, with the class of 1915, he was enrolled into the infantry first like everybody else, then by selection into the air force. Benoist witnessed the birth of the fighter, but he was so skilled that he was soon initiating the others in acrobatics, a vital element of aerial combat.

He was twenty-three when peace returned; contests continued, but more peaceful versions this time, in the form of racing cycle-cars. These were light, primitive machines whose underpowered engines needed deft handling, and the weak brakes a certain temperament. Robert Benoist, who had done his basic training, was soon spotted for his skill and natural elegance by Louis Delâge, who raced his cars under the same name (but without the accent, which he thought was too French for the export market). He graduated to big machines and very big competitions, against the best drivers of the day, and Benoist got a taste of racing in its prime, with all the success and also bereavement that it entailed at the time. Montlhéry was his first Grand Prix win, which coincided with the death of Antonio Ascari round the fast bend that has borne his name ever since. After the race, Benoist placed his laurel wreath on the spot where his rival's Alfa Romeo overturned.

There were a lot of deaths. At the Targa Florio in 1926, Count Giulio Masetti went off the road in his Delage Number 13. Benoist stopped to help him but only in time to witness his final look. There is a lasting superstition, in that the number 13 is never assigned to racers.

Benoist was very successful: he was racing almost every Sunday; he took part in international Grand Prix (France, Italy, England, Morocco, etc.), scrambling (driving the over-powerful Delage torpedoes), and gained records (including on ice in Norway). In 1927, Benoist claimed every Grand Prix of the year, giving the title of World Champion to his employer (it wasn't yet awarded to the drivers themselves).

The winning racing driver: Robert Benoist and his Delage won all the major Grand Prix of the 1927 season (facing page).

At the height of his success, Benoist withdrew and ran a garage in Paris. To inaugurate it, he organized a race up and down the ramp between the floors, which he won. After four quiet years in management, Benoist resigned and "relapsed." He signed up with Bugatti, as both salesman of these prestigious vehicles and driver. On the Bugattis, he sometimes teamed up with Philippe de Rothschild, the son of his parents' ex-bosses. Notably, he won the 1937 Le Mans. War returned to France. The army was routed and Benoist, who had fallen back to Paris, found the Germans there. At the wheel of

his Bugatti 57 S, he attempted to escape, which led to a rather bizarre episode during which his car was requisitioned by the Germans and Benoist found himself in an armored column; nevertheless, he managed to get away and shake off his pursuers, who unsurprisingly failed to catch the former world racing champion!

After the Armistice was signed, Benoist was at once contacted by William Grover-Williams, a former chauffeur and the first winner of the 1929 Monaco Grand Prix. The Anglo-Frenchman had been dropped into France to organize "Chestnut," a resistance network made up of racing drivers

Pictured in 1935, Benoist at the wheel of a Bugatti Type 59 (left). Under the bonnet was an eight-cylinder inline engine, a compressor, 250 bhp for 750 kg. Much more than 250 kph but still cable brakes!

and personnel, including Benoist, Jean-Pierre Wimille, and Robert Mazaud. The focal center was Benoist's parents' home in Auffargis, and it was there that Grover-Williams was arrested in 1943. Tortured and deported, he was very likely executed at Sachsenhausen. Arrested a few days later in Paris, Benoist jumped out of a moving Gestapo Traction and managed to get away along the Passage des Princes.

Benoist was eventually smuggled out of France to Great Britain, where he was made a captain in the British army, and was then dropped back into France to set up and run the

"Clergyman" network, which carried out acts of resistance and sabotage. A few weeks later, the Feldgendarmerie caught him once again. This time it was his skills as a former cycling champion that proved useful: he made his getaway by pedaling off on a policeman's bike.

But on June 18, 1944, he was arrested once again. Securely guarded, he was taken to Gestapo headquarters where he was interrogated for a fortnight. He was deported to Buchenwald where he was shot a few months later. The first race organized after the war, in the Bois de Boulogne, was called the Robert Benoist Cup.

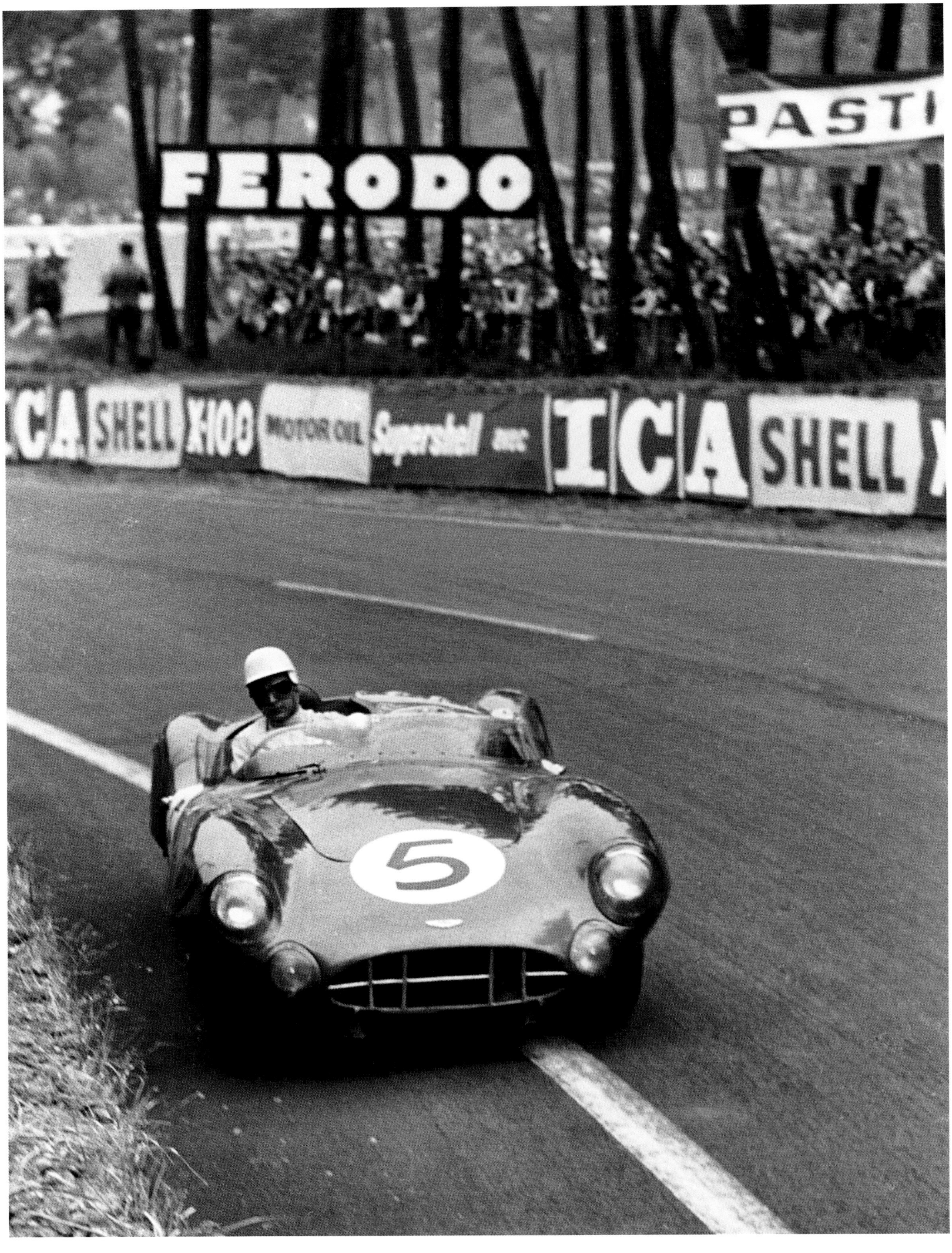
PASTI
FERODO
SHELL
X-100
MOTOR OIL
Supershell
ICA
SHELL
5

The Fifties

Spotlights

The miracle had become commonplace, and now everybody had their own car, or could dream of having one. The car industry had never been so important; it symbolized the free world: one way of life rather than another. Work and you'll have a car. Succeed and you'll have an even more beautiful one. In this widely motorized world, the enthusiasts distinguished themselves by driving further, more forcefully, or differently. The postwar artists, who took their introspection everywhere, invented a new indolence and were as at home in their car as if it had been their own bedroom—one which could move around. It's through a windscreen that you could discover the world; it's through a windscreen that the world could see you.

Drivers had never been such prodigies, nor so often in danger. Each racing season, each racing weekend, produced new records, but also new tragedies.

And this fervor wasn't showing any sign of flagging.

John Cobb
Alfonso de Portago
Harley J. Earl
Paul Frère
Preston Tucker
Mike Hawthorn
John Cooper
James Dean
Giovanni Agnelli
Françoise Sagan
Juan Manuel Fangio
Enzo Ferrari

John Cobb

1899-1952

Highlander

Drivers normally aim to beat their peers, and that's usually good enough for them. As for John Cobb, though, he always wanted to go further than that. From races he turned to speed records, becoming the ultimate record-breaker of his generation.

For lovers of speed, the center of the British world was how you might describe Brooklands, the track to the south of London, from 1907 to 1939. It was the first autodrome in the world; it had high, cambered bends so that you could keep the speed you'd reached in the straights, reduce braking and let power take over. People raced each other, according to their own and local rules. Every Saturday the track attracted car-owning gentlemen smitten with the speed bug, and the local urchins who came to deafen themselves with the roar of the engines. Eventually belonging to the former group, John Rhodes Cobb for a while belonged among the latter. Born at Esher, about 6 miles (10 km) from the track, he'd go there on his bicycle.

Since he had to grow, he grew a lot. He was tall, and a bit plump; he wasn't the sort of driver who'd be happy fooling around on a Morgan tricycle with ground-down cylinder heads. He had to have something solid, a big car, just fast. At Brooklands, Class A designated the class of automobile with more than 8,000 cc (8-liter) engines. Just as a reminder: the engine in the average modern car engine is less than 2,000 cc (2 liters). On the approaches to the circuit, traders and craftsmen supplied the gentlemen with all they needed to win. By 1933, John Cobb had become wealthy as the manager of a fur brokerage company.

He was a good client. Reid Railton designed a very special chassis for him on which he installed a Napier engine: twelve cylinders in three rows of four, 24 liters, almost 600 bhp and 2,200 rpm. If the engine had been a clock it would have been Big Ben, if it had been a monkey it would have been King Kong and if it had been a fish it would have been Moby Dick. In the case in point, it was an enormous aircraft engine, inspired by the excitement of the race, and the rather vain but very natural desire to own the biggest machine.

The mechanic's thrill was in creating a machine unlike any other; the driver's thrill was in chasing sensations unlike any he had experienced before, with his eyes on the huge rev counter where the red zone began at 2,200 rpm, his right foot regulating the flow of fuel into the twelve huge cavities, operated by the central pedal; the brake was on the right of the accelerator. It was like a safe combination dial for the uninitiated: those taking part in high-speed driving required a certain amount of savvy. This same pedal only controlled two drums on the rear wheels: no front brakes. To win its races, the Napier-Railton relied only on its huge power, more than 500 bhp, enough to complete and win the 312.5 mph (500 km/h) at Brooklands, 113 laps, burning up between 130 and 160 gallons (500 and 600 liters) of

Le Mans 24 Hours, 1957: the Whitehead brothers' Aston Martin negotiating the Ss (p. 82).

John Cobb at the wheel of his Crusader (facing page). Breaking speed records was a matter of having the physical courage needed to push the throttle at exactly the right moment, but also, during the preparation, having the courage to go through with the attempt.

fuel; around 32 gallons (120 liters) for a hundred kilometers was a nice figure but not as nice as the almost 127.5 mph (204 km/h) average speed. The Napier-Railton sailed past its competitors. Then Cobb returned to the track alone and set the absolute record for one lap—an average of 143.44 mph (230.84 km/h)—on October 7, 1935.

But it wasn't enough. John Cobb wanted to go even faster and for that he took his monster to the States, to the Great Salt Lake at Bonneville, a straight and uncluttered track where he clocked up 168.73 mph (269.98 km/h), which was fantastic in 1935. Was he satisfied? Of course he wasn't—for competitive people, these drives merely demand they go further.

Cobb ordered a new car from Reid Railton, onto which he could fit a new 12-cylinder Napier, coupled to another, identical one, producing 48,000 cc, more than 1,000 bhp. The driver had become a sort of a tightrope walker, balancing on speed, constantly running faster on thinner and thinner cables, reaching 350.194 mph (563 km/h) in 1938 and 369.741 mph (591.58 km/h) in 1939. John Cobb was designated the fastest man on earth.

Cobb spent the war years flying planes, first in the Royal Air Force and then for the Air Transport Auxiliary; then in 1947, he married Elizabeth Mitchell-Smith, late in life at forty-eight. Cobb returned to Bonneville to defend his land-speed record, reaching 396.25 mph (634 km/h).

His prowess at the wheel was far more than just technical skill. The speed that the driver reached, represented by a few decimals in the newspaper and sometimes followed by exclamation marks, in fact involved a very physical, vibrating reality, a peril which had to be faced and overcome. In the hostile air, and its brutal swirling backwash, these pioneers had to bore their way through, getting closer and closer to the speed of the earth's rotation. They needed immense courage to fuel the fire of this devil's cauldron, perched atop an increasingly frail vehicle. It must have been a source of constant concern during the long preparations for the brief and astounding explosion of speed.

After just fourteen months' marriage, his wife Elizabeth died. John Cobb, a naturally taciturn figure, was not one to open his heart a great deal, but he staggered under the blow. However, in 1950 he met Vera Victoria Henderson and married her. Reid Railton got in touch with him again: he wanted to design a record-breaking boat and he was determined that John Cobb would pilot it. But first it had to be financed.

Fifteen thousand pounds were spent before the boat could even be put on the water. It was still powered by an aircraft engine, a De Havilland Ghost jet turbine. As a venue for the record attempts, they chose the black, calm waters of Loch Ness, 23 miles (37 km) long and a thousand feet deep. In 1952, John Rhodes Cobb, still pursuing the dragon of speed, sliced the surface of Loch Ness with the bows of his *Crusader* and pushed down on the throttle. He reached over 200 mph (320 km/h), but the boat skewed and exploded, killing Cobb; the knight ultimately vanquished by the dragon.

It flies! The Napier-Railton, heavy but very powerful, bounces off the cambered bends at Brooklands at more than 125 mph.

John Cobb.

Racing cars are only good for going round at the highest speeds; in particular the Aero Engine Racing Cars, single-seaters fitted with aircraft engines (above).

The Railton Mobil Special (left), which achieved 396 mph in 1947. Twice 24 cylinders and 1,000 bhp. The vehicle becomes a sort of deep-sea diving suit that extends the driver's movements.

Alfonso de Portago

1928-1957

The Guest

What is it that makes rich people, or aristocrats, drive in races? When you have everything, why risk everything? For Alfonso de Portago, the ending was tragic, but the story itself was a huge adventure.

Luck is basically unfair, otherwise it wouldn't be luck. The circumstances of birth favored Alfonso de Portago, a direct descendant of the conquistador, Alvar Núñez Cabeza de Vaca, who discovered the Iguazú Falls in Brazil. Alfonso was King Alfonso XIII's godson and nonchalantly bore the titles of marquis and Spanish grandee. He was born in London, and enjoyed everything an international playboy might expect: good physique, money, dilettantism (but definitely not laziness); for this sporting enthusiast was an excellent swimmer, had ridden in the very difficult Aintree Grand National Steeplechase, and was well regarded in the best polo teams. But this laid-back aristocrat did not really go in for sophisticated attire; more often than not, he wore a leather jacket and canvas trousers—very much a sportsman's attire, in days when social classes were distinguished by what people wore. He allowed himself to be called "Fon," much less of a mouthful than "Alfonso Cabeza de Vaca de Carvajal, Marquis of Portago and Count of Mejorada," his full patronymic.

Fon was perhaps a few decades ahead of the time when people finally abandoned etiquette—which did cause some mix-ups. Bernard Cahier, a great international car sports photographer, recalls this eventful passage through New York customs: "The customs officer was watching this unshaven man surreptitiously until he showed him his diplomatic passport. The official nearly had an attack!" Richard von Frankenberg, the German driver and journalist had the same experience. With a friend in the stands at Monza, they were wondering what that "Italian mechanic" was doing there before seeing him getting into a brand-new Thunderbird in which a blonde model was waiting for him.

The marquis found it difficult to pass up cars. Firstly because—when you have everything—they are one of the rare really new things that money could buy; then because driving them presupposed he could master them and would challenge the sportsman in him, the son of a golf, polo, and sailing champion. However Portago did not take up car racing initially. He was a horseman first, competing in equestrian events at an international level.

Fon met Harry Schell, an American in Paris, who drove for Maserati and Gordini in Formula 1. He initiated him into the art of driving. Portago had another transcontinental friendship with Luigi Chinetti, three-time winner at Le Mans and a friend of Enzo Ferrari, and who took the Ferrari virus to the Americas. Chinetti took him on as his teammate—i.e. his passenger, not a very nice position, once you know that it was a question of racing in the Pan-American, the fastest and most dangerous of the great competitions of the times. It was a race by stages, during which Fon was relieved when they had to give up on the third day because of a breakdown. But the whole business had got him very interested. He bought himself a black Ferrari 735 S and started

Money, charm, beautiful cars, the good life. But the Marquis of Portago (facing page) also wanted to go fast.

to take part in international races himself; though the level of these was not very high, although one or two authentic champions could be found chasing the prize money.

It was in the Caracas Grand Prix in Venezuela that he really set himself up as a star. No doubt not all the cream of the racing drivers had taken the trouble to cross the Atlantic, but Fangio was there and Fon finished second behind the Argentinean and his factory Maserati. In the Nassau Grand Prix, in the Bahamas, he won; this was important because the race was followed by the American public, who were Ferrari's leading customers.

Then a new friend, Edmund Nelson, a boxing champion, introduced him to the noble sport, as well as to bobsleighing, which meant speed again, and going downhill fast, with just a bit of control. Portago was so keen that he founded the Spanish Olympic team in that discipline, and just missed a medal the 1956 Cortina d'Ampezzo games. "In exchange," Portago got Nelson involved in the adventure of the automobile Tour de France, on a production series Ferrari: they won it.

Enzo Ferrari had Portago's name transferred from his customers' list to that of his official drivers. Joining the Scuderia (Italian for "stable") was a great honor, and he definitely took his task very seriously. For the young marquis, being part of this carefully selected elite represented a noble title of another kind: one which he had had to earn for himself and that he would not be able to keep forever.

Obviously not as fast as Fangio or Collins, Portago's initial results were nonetheless very respectable, particularly when racing at that level. At Silverstone he equaled Behra's time in a Maserati and had an excellent race, which had him fourth after two hours, behind Moss, Fangio, and Collins. But Collins had broken his engine, so he borrowed Portago's car. At the time the pecking order in the team was clear. It is difficult to know what Fon thought of the incident. At Monza, Portago, who was definitely fast on the fastest tracks, qualified less than two seconds behind Collins, but when the tread came off a tire at high speed, damaging his suspension, he had to abandon the race; he was seventh. Taking big strides, Fon became more and

Cigarette hanging from his lips, wearing an open-necked shirt, slightly disheveled, the Spanish grandee invented a new genre: the relaxed playboy.

more professional and held onto his place bravely. In 1957 he discovered new circuits; first of all Buenos Aires, where he finished fifth just behind Harry Schell; and then the incredibly difficult Mille Miglia: 1,000 miles (1,600 km) of roads, lined with dense crowds, snaking through the Italian mountains. Fon was wary of this race in which he had everything to lose as he risked being outdone by the Belgian Gendebien driving a less powerful Ferrari. Everything went well until about 60 miles (100 km) from the end: was it a puncture, a mechanical breakdown, or was it perhaps driver error? Sometimes it just happens that a car goes off the road. When people get involved in a sport, when they reach the pinnacle of that sport, it is through the mistakes they make that you are suddenly made all too aware of the difficulties they face and paradoxically how good they are. There was no second chance for Fon, though, or for his co-driver Edmund Nelson; tragically they killed ten

spectators when their car spun out of control. The Mille Miglia was never organized again.

During an interview, which had been recorded some months earlier, you can hear Portago answering the usual question about how he felt about fatal accidents: "On the Sunday of the accident, you remain dumbfounded. How stupid these races are! The next day, you're still thinking about it and you conclude that it'd be better if you gave up racing. The fact that you're still safe and sound is reassuring. It would be cowardly to abandon now in mid-season. We'll think about it at the end of the season, perhaps. On Tuesday, you're no longer thinking about the accident but about the forthcoming races."

This brave dilettante had taken speed as his kingdom and his mission had been to go and protect its far-distant marches, at the extreme limits of his talent. He might have lacked ability but never courage.

The first season driving single-seaters for "Fon" de Portago, here at the Pau Grand Prix, 1955, in which he finished eighth.

Harley J. Earl
1893-1969

The Power of Drawing

We all know the power of weapons, of laws, and of words. Harley J. Earl cultivated the power of drawing. Chief designer at the world's foremost car manufacturer, General Motors, this is the man who imposed his tastes, his intuitions, and his whims on drivers all over the world.

In traffic jams, even the most beautiful cars are reduced to the same level as all the others and their drivers forced to be humble. But Harvey J. Earl managed to find a way to feel superior to all his comrades-in-traffic-jams: all around him, in 1950s America, a good half of the vehicles held up at each traffic light owed their outline to him. It was a strange feeling of power: in the eternal playground arguments about the beauty of cars, he would always have the last word: "I'm the one who made that." He could look down at his credulous contemporaries who were quite happy to spend a few extra dollars for a new bit of chrome-work, a bit like a hook-salesman reigning over a community of fishermen.

Born in 1893 in Hollywood of a coach-worker father, Harley became familiar early on with tailor-made cars for cinema people, without being afraid of overdoing things: the actor Tom Mix, for instance, as the undisputed king of the silent Western, had ordered a star-studded limousine complete with TM armories and a real saddle on the roof. Harley J. Earl met Alfred Sloan, General Motors' boss, who was looking for a way to wrongfoot Henry Ford's over-standardized, but nonetheless very profitable, creations. He offered

Earl the very first stylist's office ever created by a car firm, the "art and color department." Earl soon made it into his command platform and then reigned over Detroit from 1927 to 1959.

Harley Earl was a big man, more than six feet (1.90 m) tall; he also had a big mouth and a large-caliber opinion of himself. Under his well-rounded, elegantly balding skull, were tomorrow's unattainable plans.

He took over the future, using it as an extra weapon to hone his clientele's greediness. He designed unique models, on which he tested new, increasingly emphatic and daring shapes. These dream cars were often given groundbreaking solutions (automatic gearboxes, turbine engines, etc.) or exclusive options like photoelectric cells switching on the headlights (nicely christened "twilight sentinel"), automatic hoods, etc. Many of the innovations now installed in today's cars were actually thought up for the dream cars of the fifties and sixties. There were even automatic jacks, for which we are still waiting, fifty years later!

What's· more, these dream cars were exhibited in fairs or at—another of Earl's inventions—traveling "motoramas," and aroused the interest of the public, who were becoming

After the war, the United States was the center of the world, and the car was its center of gravity. Harley Earl (facing page), who presided over the destinies of millions of cars, was the international arbiter of elegance.

increasingly aware of the aesthetics of the bodywork. Under his impulsion, GM deliberately put its cars "out of fashion" from one model to the next to stimulate turnover among its clientele. The other makers had to react and ape his practices. During the reign of Harley J. Earl, who was capable—merely by redesigning the radiator grill—of improving the sales curve of a particular model, and the company's stock exchange price, style became the most important force driving sales. Technical progress, which was far more costly, could now slow down.

In 1951, Earl designed two masterly dream cars, the XP-300 and the Sabre, for Buick, one of General Motors' makes. Earl gave the first to Batman; it was painted black and sported bats on yellow backgrounds and became cinema's first Batmobile. He kept the second, an ineffable sky-blue cabriolet, to commute the 14 miles between his home in Touraine Street in the classy Grosse-Pierre district and Detroit, where his office was. It was a huge office, with massive, fluid, oblong, wooden, and aluminum furniture, shaped like an aircraft wing or superb coachwork, made by the Swedish designer Eero Saarinen.

Mr. Earl had also become a legend. The American press nicknamed him MisterI, which was the sort of name given to those superheroes whose rise within Marvel Comics accompanied his own: Superman (1938), Batman (1939), the Fantastic Four (1956), and so on. If the cartoonists had had the idea of inventing a "Supercarman," he would certainly have had some of Earl's powers.

So the master of Detroit was just a kid like us, a show-off who wanted to be admired in an astonishing car. Fifty-five years later, there is still a lingering doubt: and what if Harley J. Earl had misappropriated General Motors' life blood, subverted its general staff, squandered its subsidies, just so he could have his own dream car every year?

There again, he was a good ambassador for his country. A French or Italian worker going to the cinema on Saturday night, then admiring Earl's creatures at the car show on Sunday, would be less likely to heed anti-American views during Monday's union cell meeting. Was the Sabre a propaganda tool? Oh yes, even the name—French—so as to be chic, but also the same name as the F-86 Sabre, the jet fighter "defending the free world" in Korea.

So what Earl was he, Mr. Harley? Was he an authoritarian and pragmatic boss, a stylist with unlimited inspiration, an impenitent hedonist, or a propagandist for the American way of life?

Paul Frère
1917-2008

Special Correspondent

Sports and automobile racing journalists usually report enthusiastically, sometimes enviously, from the sidelines. Paul Frère didn't. He drew the information for his readers from right behind the steering wheel, first hand.

Racing driver is a job that many people would love to have. Paul Frère was able to experience the pleasure of driving the most powerful and most successful machines of his time, like Aston Martin DBR1, Porsche RAK, Jaguar D, Ferrari Testarossa, and even some Formula 1 racers like the Lancia-Ferrari D50. But driving was not his principal job. He was actually an automobile journalist, again an occupation that many people would envy. After World War II, and for more than fifty years, Frère published his reviews of trials in his country's press (he was Belgian) but also in France, America, Germany, and Japan. His writing produced a rather unique mixture of driving impressions that would be utterly worthy of a racing driver, and of extremely specialized technical considerations, backed by sensible observations for improving car racing. For writing had not been his first career choice either. He was in fact an engineer by background. So he could wear three different hats on that clever head of his.

Paul Frère was born in Brussels in 1917, but it wasn't until 1948 that he managed to get behind the steering wheel of a racing car. He was already a family man, so envisaging a change of jobs was risky, for at the time racing drivers' salaries were not what they can be nowadays—far from it. Paul keenly accepted the opportunity but he wisely also continued with his "real," main

bread-winning jobs. He was very much sought after and his career was that of the most titled amateur ever seen racing. He was above all a specialist, dreaded by his adversaries on the Le Mans and Spa-Francorchamps circuits, where the Belgian Grand Prix was held.

In the Fifties, you didn't join Formula 1 preceded by a press campaign, nor did you have a three-year contract drawn up by umpteen lawyers. Frère was able to drive in his own national Grand Prix because he'd been brilliant in the lower groupings, each time in one race only. However, on the impressive course at Spa, Frère "won himself some points" three times: in 1952 for his very first Grand Prix where he came in fifth in an HWM. In 1954 he was fourth in a Ferrari Supersqualo. In 1956 Ferrari got in touch with him but he played hard to get: he hadn't driven a single-seater for a year and thought he wouldn't do well. He nonetheless came second, just behind Peter Collins, his leader in the Scuderia.

In his memoirs, *My Terrible Joys*,[1] the great Enzo presented a gallery of portraits of the drivers he had raced. In one chapter, entitled "*Piloti, che gente!*" (Drivers, what people!)—an exclamation in which you can detect his admiration but also his envious exasperation with all these young people he counted on to make his colors triumph but who in fact had taken his place behind the wheel—Ferrari wrote the following: "Frère is such

So that wasn't too difficult, was it?: the superior calm of the man in the cockpit, Paul Frère (facing page).

a good driver and journalist that it is impossible to know which is his first job." This was rare praise indeed from the man who, a few pages later, decried a certain Juan Manuel Fangio.

Paul was a Le Mans specialist. He took part for the first time in 1953 with a factory 1,500 given him by the recently formed Porsche team; he won his class with Richard von Frankenberg who, like him, was primarily a pen pusher, but in German. The year 1955 was the tragic one at Le Mans, in which Levegh's Mercedes exploded in the crowd, killing eighty-two spectators. The race continued, however, and, imperturbable in the ensuing grim mood, Frère came in second in his Jaguar. It was also at Le Mans in 1956 that he made "the biggest mistake of [his] life"—in his own words—during the second lap. He slewed round on the soaking bend at Tertre Rouge, causing a pile-up, galling in one who was usually so consistent. His Jaguar had to be withdrawn, as did Fairman's and the Marquis de Portago's Ferrari. Fourth in 1957 and 1958 in a Jaguar D Type, then Porsche RSK, he was

runner-up in the 1959 event, giving the Aston Martins a historic double.

In 1960 he triumphed with his fellow-Belgian Olivier Gendebien in a Ferrari. It was a triumph that almost turned into a disaster. Wanting that year to associate racing cars with road GTs, the Automobile Club de l'Ouest imposed much higher windscreens. On the Tipo 61 Birdcages, Maserati interpreted the rule to the letter and the windscreen became a sloping surface of Plexiglass, beginning just behind the radiator grill. Ferrari dealt with problem disdainfully by only increasing the height of the usual screen frame. A mere detail, was it? The aerodynamic impact was huge, so much so that—before the first relay—three Testarossas gave up, having run out of fuel. Frère had succeeded in rallying the stand. He recalls in his memoirs: "At Les Hunaudières, the Maserati, which was much better profiled, left us behind. I timed our Testarossa at only [162.5 mph] 260 km/h [behind the driver, the journalist-tester was trying to be precise and put

a figure to his impressions]; the only thing we could do was wait for the Maserati to abandon, which wasn't long in coming."[2] A few years later, when Frère was himself interviewed, he told how he had given Ferrari his precious observations as a driver-engineer:

"I went to Maranello to thank him."

"He thanked you too, I'd have thought, no?"

"Oh, him? No, he never thanked anybody! I told him he needed to make the windscreens aerodynamic. He took me by the shoulder and said with that fatherly, slightly patronizing tone of his: 'You know, Frère, aerodynamics and all that, it's for people who can't make an engine.' You could never explain anything to Mr. Ferrari."

Back on the 1960 Le Mans podium, Frère savored his success. Except that he had promised his wife and his three daughters that he would stop his escapades with beautiful racing cars, so that this consecration was also the end of his career, the end and the summit, the perfect definition of an apotheosis.

Retiring from racing didn't mean giving up cars. On the contrary, his job as a journalist took him every year to the Le Mans 24 Hours to observe, to cover and comment on both the sport and the technical innovation aspects of it. He wrote a book about the race, which is still in print today. And it was again at Le Mans in 2003 that, at Audi's invitation, while trying out a modern R LMP 1 for a Japanese TV channel, he astounded all the young drivers by clocking up a time which would have qualified him for the middle of the grid. He was eighty-six.

1. Enzo Ferrari, *My Terrible Joys,* Hamish Hamilton Ltd., 1963.
2. Paul Frère, *Les 800 Heures, Le Mans 1923–1966,* Editions du Palmier, 2005. (Our translation)

"You don't know what to think of Frère, who is as good a journalist as he is a driver," as Enzo Ferrari used to say. Special correspondent at the highest speeds, Paul Frère here finishes runner-up in the 1959 Le Mans 24 Hours.

Preston Tucker

1903-1956

Turbocharged Tucker

Preston Tucker was an innovator. In 1945, he yearned to shape postwar America and dreamed of it in his own image: enthusiastic, and searching for transformation through technology. But the authorities thought differently.

"The only really new car for fifty years!" was his publicity slogan, which was a bold claim, especially as cars had only been around for fifty years or so anyway. Preston Tucker was only forty-three and he had just set up his own company, which was supposed to be bringing out a revolutionary car within twelve months, rendering all that had gone before outmoded, and yet for a price comparable to conventional cars, for which the capital investment had been written off ages ago.

The Tucker was a real engineer's car, full of ideas. It was streamlined and light because it was made of aluminum; it was low-slung, and nothing in its appearance was quite normal. The doors cut out a large section of the roof. There were three headlights, one of which was right in the center of the hood and followed the steering wheel's movements. All the controls were regrouped behind the steering wheel and padding protected the passengers in case of a collision. The rear finished in a slight slope and opened to reveal the engine. This was an enormous flat-six, placed transversally so there was no need for transmission or even gearboxes. Add independent wheels, hydraulic shock absorbers, and very special disk brakes.

The "Tucker Torpedo," as it was popularly known, with its mountain of innovations, recalled the Citroën Traction of 1934. Indeed he had a lot of things in common with that other innovator,

André Citroën, like his taste for publicity, and his love of new ideas. Both the American and the Frenchman exhibited that curious mixture of commercial predator and progressive militant. Some of their bold ideas gradually fell by the wayside as the prototypes got closer to the production series, and this was just as true for the Citroën Traction as it was for the Tucker '48 (Tucker Torpedo). Already the pre-production series Torpedo '48 was less radical than expected but there was still enough for the car to have real personality and be a true commercial success.

But the big three in Detroit (General Motors, Chrysler Corporation, Ford Motor Company) had taken stock of the potential dangers that lay ahead. They had decided that if the postwar period turned out to be an opportunity for too much technological progress, it would upset everybody, so they reached an agreement to stifle their respective research departments' wishes. As for Tucker, the factory sites he tried to buy mysteriously slipped through his fingers; a smear campaign in the press caused his new company's share price to fall; and the Inland Revenue charged him with fraud: it seemed that Tucker had no means of delivering his marvel. Eventually Tucker was acquitted of all charges, but during the long court case his finances collapsed, and the Tucker '48 was never produced. Automobile history might have been very different.

Hats off, Mr. Tucker (facing page): your car is beautiful, entirely new, and it almost existed for real....

Mike Hawthorn
1929–1959

Hell's Angel

The racing driver is first and foremost a man who dares to do what our caution forbids us to. You need skill, determination, and perhaps even a little selfishness.

The rumor goes that in England there are as many pubs as there are clubs, and as many circuits as there are farms. This is surely a bit exaggerated, but what is certain is that postwar Britain had numerous racing tracks. The countless airfields that the RAF built to scatter its forces and thwart German air raids were no longer used; they became concrete tracks where you could happily try out your MG at weekends. All you needed were a few mates and a timekeeper, and races could flourish. It was the breeding ground for the British domination of automobile sports, still to be felt sixty years on in Formula 1, and Mike Hawthorn was the typical product of this environment. But he had had a head's start: his father, Leslie Hawthorn, was a garage owner and demonstrator, and opened the Tourist Trophy Garage in 1932, where he sold secondhand Lancia Lambdas and did up cars and motorbikes for racing.

Near Brooklands, the first real autodrome in the world, built in 1907, Leslie's only son, Mike, was constantly under the customers' feet, always wheeling around them on his bicycle and making loud engine sounds with his mouth. It would be something of an understatement to say he'd been bitten by the speed bug. He was himself like a bug, born out of the swirl of dirty oil and grease, gearbox oil, and drivers' bragging. Speed would be his biotope: he would be a racing driver.

At fifteen he had begun riding an old James Villiers motorbike. His father faked his age so he could obtain his license. The bike was followed by a Fiat Topolino. Hardly what you would call powerful, but its road-holding was well balanced; he took bends "like Nuvolari." Did he ever actually learn to drive? There was no need. He was one of those who already knew how to.

Bikes, boozing, and birds were the glorious trio that constituted a happy adolescence. On the side, Mike studied mechanical engineering on a sandwich course and became an apprentice with Dennis Brothers. And above all he raced, trialing and scrambling, threatening to enter the 500 cc category riding a BSA 350.

His bike was therefore as much a sport as a means of transport, and a way of impressing the girls and his mates. For the girls, his helmeted, fair-haired, six-foot-three frame seemed to be enough. To impress his mates, Mike would ride his bike on and along the wall at Dennis Bros. The lad was skillful and fast, enough to make his father dream; so he got hold of two Rileys and set off to put them down for Dundrod. The son won his race; his father was runner-up in his. It was a big moment. A series of little victories followed. Hawthorn's impeccable beginnings attracted people's attention, and one of his father's friends had a single-seat Cooper Bristol built for him.

This ended the sense of expectancy. Hawthorn the novice was straightaway the fastest of the Cooper drivers, and for his first real competition, the Goodwood 1952 Easter Cups,

Mike Hawthorn cut a glamorous figure with his blond good looks and his skill as a driver (facing page).

he won two races and finished runner-up in the third. There was just one small detail: there were two Argentinean drivers on the starting grid: Froilàn Gonzalez and Juan Manuel Fangio. But they weren't driving their usual mounts. Fangio was trying out a Cooper, like Mike, but wasn't used to it; neither was he familiar with the track, and only finished fifth. In the other race, reserved for Formula 1, Gonzalez won driving a 4.5-liter Thinwall Special against which Mike only had his 2-liter Cooper. He was runner-up, only 26 seconds behind the winner.

He was put down for the 1952 Grand Prix. His baptism of fire was at Spa, the 8.75-mile (14 km) circuit in the Ardennes, where of course it rained and in which he finished fourth behind Ascari, Taruffi, and Manzon, but in front of Prince Bira, Lance Macklin, Johnny Claes.

At Silverstone he won a podium place behind the inaccessible Ferraris! He was only twenty-three years old. His manner, his youth, his shining smile and his town clothes, which he insisted on wearing when racing, all very quickly built up a legend around him. He'd earned his place in Formula 1 and his career was by now all marked out: in 1953 he was with Ferrari and won at Rheims, battling it out with Fangio's Maserati for the whole of the race.

Like all Grand Prix racing drivers, Mike also took part in endurance races. At Le Mans in 1955, he went through the best and the worst, the best being victory and the worst being accused of dangerous driving. At the beginning of the race he was battling it out with his Jaguar D Type against Fangio's Mercedes 300 SLR. They both left everybody way behind them. After two hours, Hawthorn was leading, with Fangio in his wake, fifty yards behind him. In the long, fast, and misleadingly straight line leading from Arnage to the stands, he lapped the other Mercedes, carrying Kling and Levegh. Mike had to make a pit stop; he then overtook Macklin's little Austin Healey, cut in front of it and stood on his powerful disc brakes. Macklin swerved and cut out in front of Levegh's Mercedes, which had topped well over 150 mph (240 km/h). Levegh roared up the MG's ski-jump-shaped rear; it spun out of control at full speed, crossed the track and killed an official in the stands. Levegh was already dead; his Mercedes broke up, one half burning on the fascines, the other—the engine and the front axle—somersaulted into the crowd, causing more than eighty-seven casualties.

Twenty-two hours later, Jaguar, Mike Hawthorn (and Ivor Bueb) came in triumphant. The usual photographs were taken of the team smiling under the laurel wreaths. But at the cataclysmic moment just after the accident, Hawthorn fled from the stand, extremely distressed; the men in his team had to find him first and then comfort him before he agreed to carry on with the race. Many held him responsible; some found other causes for the drama, blaming Levegh's lack of reflexes, or the Mercedes' fuel, which seemed to have exploded. Some countries subsequently suspended all motor competitions. The controversy in some ways has continued right up to this day.

From the moral standpoint, it's hard to say, but whoever risks his life so tangibly every weekend moves about in a special world: to feel sorry for yourself would be a sign of weakness and an added danger. Mike himself had already had a spell in hospital. In the 1954 Syracuse Grand Prix, he brushed against a wall, tearing off the fuel tank cap. Blazing gas was sprayed all over him while he was still driving, and both his legs and his left arm were seriously burnt. But he resumed racing as soon as he could, for he earned his living with the prize money and he had to pay the Scuderia Ferrari back, since they had paid all the hospital fees for him. On a rainy night two months later, Mike's father was killed on the Goodwood Road at Farnham at the wheel of his Lancia Aurelia B20. His mother, Winifred, looked after the garage so that Mike could remain based at Maranello.

In 1957, Mike came across his old friend Peter Collins. Both of them gave the Maseratis a hard time and it took all Fangio's skills to outdo them, once again on the Nürburgring merry-go-round. In 1958, Mike won the title of World Champion, the first Englishman to do so. He succeeded the maestro, Fangio (five World Championship titles, of which four were in consecutive years) and was once again a hero for his supporters, who had been criticizing him for getting out of doing military service. But the season had been a hard one. Luigi Musso, Mike's teammate with Ferrari, was runner-up at Monaco, and battled with him for the best time at Rheims. Then, in the same French Grand Prix, Musso was killed. Hawthorn won and Fangio announced that he was going to hang up his gloves.

At Silverstone, it was Peter Collins who won with Hawthorn hard on his heels, making a British double for their own Grand Prix. A fortnight later, Mike got his revenge at Nürburgring, chalking up

the best times during the trials. Peter was only fourth; but the Ferraris led during the race. Tony Brooks in his Vanwall managing nonetheless to overtake them! It was a superb fight. Then suddenly Peter's red Ferrari went off course, left the track and hit a tree: Peter died. In the same lap Hawthorn's engine broke and he gave up. Three further Grand Prix followed. Oporto: Hawthorn was runner-up to Moss. Monza: Hawthorn was runner-up to Brooks. At Casablanca it was all suspense. For Moss to win the title, Moss had to win the race and Hawthorn not be second. But Moss's teammates, whose job it was to slip in between them, broke down one after the other. The last, Stuart Lewis-Evans, a twenty-eight-year-old Englishman, was trying to move up when his gearbox seized up. The Vanwall left the track and burst into flames. Mike was second behind Moss so he was World Champion. Lewis-Evans was brought back by plane to England but succumbed to his injuries six days later. A short while later, Mike announced he was going to retire.

The champion, now at the summit of his art, returned to where he had started: his father's garage. But his father was no longer there. He had to build up his life again, but with what?

On January 29, 1959, it was raining. Mike started off on a day of meetings and other official business. He set off in his very special Jaguar "Mk 1." There were gusts of rain with very strong winds. At a crossroads he ran into the Mercedes 300SL belonging to the racing driver Rob Walker. It was impossible not to know whose it was; its number plates were "Rob 2." Their encounter immediately broke into a race. They sped like whirlwinds way over 100 mph (160 km/h), past the Dennis Bros workshops where Mike had been an apprentice only a few years earlier. The two men were side by side for a few hundred yards, but then Walker must have thought it was just a bit too fast for him. Mike Hawthorn started to outdistance him, probably laughing his head off. Walker saw the Jaguar going into the following big bend at top speed, starting to take on a strange angle then suddenly spin; it then hit the embankment, wrapped itself around a tree, and broke in two.

Mike was found sitting in the back seat, apparently unhurt. For him there were no more worries about his future; he had died of youth.

Zanvoort, the 1958 Dutch Grand Prix: The Ferrari Dino 246 is driven flat out by Mike Hawthorn, traditionally wearing a tie.

John Cooper
1923-2000

"Copernicus" Cooper

A revolution is perhaps the simplest way forward: send everything topsy-turvy and wrong-foot any habits. In most cases you come a cropper with that sort of thing. But when it does work, not only do you triumph, you also leave your mark on history. So it was that John Cooper upset car racing once and for all by putting the engine behind the driver.

Of course finicky historians will say all this wasn't exactly new. The American Miller had experimented with this sort of layout before the war and Ferdinand Porsche, who had designed many front-engined cars (and among the most noteworthy ones, too) considered this layout to be much better and raced the mid-engined Auto Unions. So why make Cooper the Copernicus of single-seat cars? It's just that the lessons learnt by Auto Union were more or less dropped after the war; and anyway the Auto Unions never really dominated the Mercedes and their classic layout. They could share the laurel wreaths.

On the other hand, the Coopers turned everything upside down.

John followed in his father's footsteps; with Charles Cooper he learnt how to become a mechanic and a lathe operator. The little company established in Surbiton in south-west London did up racing cars. After the war, the Coopers, father and son, very naturally started building their clients simple and economical cars which very much looked ahead to the go-kart and even the modern single-seater. These minute cars were fitted in the rear with a single-cylinder motorbike engine, a Jap 500. With rather unexpected

modesty for that world of brutes, John Cooper always maintained that his over-praised inspired insight was more common sense than anything else. By placing the engine right behind the driver, the chain-driven transmission could be retained, saving on the weight of a prop shaft. John discovered the rest with the steering wheel in his hands. It didn't drive normally, but it could be driven. It was much better balanced than a rear-engined car like the Volkswagen and much more neutral than a front-engined, rear-wheel drive car. The Cooper Jap went round bends at rather stunning speeds without batting an eyelid. It could even go faster, for what driver wouldn't go testing the limits of ground holding? An instruction book and a drastic revision of the old methods turned out to be necessary. But overall the results were brilliant and the Cooper very often won, from its first season (1948) onward. But John and Charles didn't push the idea further; first they had to climb up through the categories, using the beautiful six-cylinder Bristol engine that they mounted in the "normal order," i.e. engine, driver, and then wheel rear drive. So the revolution was therefore confined to the little 500s, getting more and more powerful and, with a Norton in place of

A genius is perhaps a very stubborn do-it-yourselfer. John Cooper aboard his record car in 1952: 26 records at stake in the 1,100 cc category.

the Jap and alcohol in place of petrol, the Cooper 500s were timed at more than 125 mph!

In 1958, John extrapolated a Formula 1 from his little cars. Despite only having a 2 200 cc engine, compared with their rivals' 2 500 cc and a handicap of 70 bhp compared with the Ferrari for example, the Cooper Climax won two victories straight off with Moss and Trintignant. A year was spent running it in and then it was the moment for the big clash, during which the Cooper was just as impressive for the spectators as it was for the participants in F1. The front-engined dinosaurs, utterly supreme a month earlier, were now devoured by these English bugs which carried off two successive world championships, in 1959 and 1960, both of them in the hands of the Australian, Jack Brabham. Soon nobody even dreamed of designing a front-engined F1 car.

John Cooper had taken over. In Great Britain he was treated as a national hero, after the earlier avalanche of Italian successes had so frustrated Union Jack supporters. But 1959 was also the year in which that other troublemaker, the featherweight Austin Mini, was launched. John Cooper, who carried on living off the cars he did up, was working on a special Dauphine into which he was trying to graft a four-cylinder Coventry Climax engine. When a production series Mini passed through his hands, he changed tactics immediately, prepared an engine and courted the managers of the giant group in order to obtain a partnership: the Mini Cooper was born from this union and took John's name to all the saloon car racetracks and rallies, especially winning the prestigious Monte Carlo rally three times. By one of history's caprices, Cooper found himself contributing to two apparently contradictory technical advances: after converting F1 to rear-engines, he then contributed enormously to the success in sport and industry of front-wheel drive for everyday cars.

Now famous, the name Cooper became a label which still survives on today's Minis, turning out royalties for John's heirs without them having to put their hands anywhere near a dirty, greasy engine or a drawing board.

Once it was created, the car lived its own—sometimes astounding—life; John Lennon at the wheel of this psychedelic Mini Cooper (left).

From time to time, racing is a brilliant universe. But there are also long days of trials on deserted circuits. Here, in 1957, a Cooper Monaco is being tested (facing page).

As for John, who was really much more of a mechanics and speed buff, the success of his cars and the need to run his companies deprived him of the joys of driving. In 1963, he couldn't resist the temptation of trying out one of his racing cars. A serious crash completed his conversion to the more peaceful duties of a company boss.

But this was also a situation that was still fraught with dangers. The habit he had of playing tricks with various mechanical bits of car led him to study a twin-engined Mini. Merging the discoveries made with the mid-engine lay-out and front wheel drive, there he was again, plunging headlong into innovation. A machine with two engines, one in the front and one in the rear, and four-wheel drive, under a Mini's silhouette! It is not known whether this eight cylinder "Twinny Mini" was designed as art for art's sake, or from a sense of fun, but it was less obviously successful. John was injured again on a motorway slip-road near Kingston trying to discover the monster's limits. This time he resolved to just drive more normal cars for getting about.

James Dean
1931-1955

Rebel Without a Chance

He was a shooting star who sparked more emotion than a thousand immobile planets. By interrupting his path when he was just taking off, Dean seems to have taken a good head start in the race towards immortality.

Jimmy was born in 1931 in America, the real one, the deepest part, as authentic as an Indiana farm could be. The saddest day of his childhood was the death of his mother when he was nine, and the most beautiful was when he was given a Whizzer motorcycle. This first machine enabled the world to open up for him. His aunt Ortense and his uncle Marcus, who brought him up, despaired of this young daredevil. "If he'd only fallen once, things might have been different," his uncle later reflected. "Trouble is, he never got hurt and he never found anything he couldn't do well almost the first time he tried it. Just one fall off the bike and maybe he'd have been afraid of speed, but he was without fear."[1]

Soon James replaced his basic mount with a Sarolea, then a Czech, which he rode lying flat out on the petrol tank, with his feet folded back up on the luggage rack.

It was obvious that he also had a taste for moving about, changing scenes, and playing roles. From acting competitions to theater classes, the person everybody described as a young rebel actually seemed to be pretty well organized.

James lived by his wits: he enrolled at the university, but only looked after the theater club there, obtained a recommendation for The Actors' Studio, a free but very selective school, acted on stage in André Gide's *Immoralist* in which he played a homosexual, which was not entirely a composition role for him; he played in commercials and television series like *The Unlighted Road*, where he played a psychopath. Slowly but surely, acting became his job. He settled near Hollywood.

His first fees paid for his motorbikes: a secondhand Triumph T110, then a new T500; next came a brand-new car: an MG TD on which he had the engine tuned up and the engine block ground down. He wrote to his girlfriend, Barbara Glenn, who had stayed in New York: "Family Dean has expanded! I have a red MG from '53. My sexual passion releases by speeding through the curves, slipping on four wheels, rapidly speeding etc. Enough opponents. My bike, my MG and my girl. I slept with my MG. We are doing it together, baby."

Girlfriend? He flitted around, flirting with both sexes, and came near to marrying an Italian starlet, Pier Angeli. But Liz Taylor, one possible conquest, wondered whether he didn't die a virgin.

It seemed that in matters of the heart, James didn't really know exactly who or where he was. But driving, he knew he liked that. He spent most nights driving up and down Mulholland Drive, a winding road that must have reminded him of his rides in Indiana and which became famous some forty-eight years later thanks to David Lynch.

Dean had money now. He fees continued to climb ($20,000 dollars for *East of Eden*, $50,000 for *Rebel Without a Cause*, $100,000 for *Giant*,

Cars fascinate those who have everything: was James Dean, here at the wheel of a Ferrari (facing page), looking for a more obvious way of displaying his talent than in Hollywood?

and soon, perhaps, he'd get $200,000 for the next film, which would put him above Marlon Brando or Montgomery Clift). He bought a white Porsche Speedster. It was because of this car that he became friendly with Wutherich, a mechanic, who initiated him into the world of racing. During one of those arduous training nights, it was again in his Speedster that he beat another record: he claimed, or was it just another rumor, to have made love to Natalie Wood, in the cramped inside of the car. Which legend should you believe?

In 1954, when he took part in his first race, Dean was not so well known. The magazines specializing in thrills for young girls had no doubt praised this upcoming star; no doubt the more serious critics had paused to review his performance in *East of Eden*, which had come out a few months earlier and which was an ambitious author's film, an epic in which Americans like to see themselves, and a big success with the public, just enough to make drivers used to competition driving sneer knowingly: "We'll eat that young snob alive." But the surprise was that James was in fact a good driver. He won his heat and, in the final the next day, it took Ken Miles, a very keen amateur and thirteen years his senior, to do James out of his victory. Ken Miles is good yardstick for us: he was a future winner at Daytona and Sebring, with a GT 40—before eventually being killed in 1966 at Riverside while testing a Ford J prototype—and gives us a good idea of what the standard of the races, and that of Jimmy, were like.

Dean was pleased with the experience and from then on he saw himself with a future in racing. He brought up the subject—surely among others—of taking ten months off from the studios to race for a whole season; meanwhile, he agreed to give up taking part in competitions for the time it took to shoot *Giant*.

Once this clause had been respected, he put himself in for the race at Salinas. He sold his white Porsche, which was a sports car that could also just as easily be used to show off along Sunset Boulevard, and bought a gray, ugly, and definitely uncomfortable racing car: unpainted bodywork, stripped of all carpets and fittings, ringing out at the slightest bit of gravel, and no windscreen. This Porsche, registered 550 RS, was more expensive

than a limousine, with that rebellious handling, light, floaty steering, and a precise engine, which only gave out its power at the top end of the rev counter. It is not known how Jimmy made out with this first real racing machine. His first concern when he got it was to paint his nickname for it on the bodywork, which was perhaps inspired by his first trial: "Little bastard."

He traveled from Los Angeles to the Salinas circuit driving this car, a custom that would be unthinkable nowadays but was quite normal then. And it was on this trip that he crashed into the blue and cream Ford Custom 50 belonging to John Turnuspeed, a young sales rep. For there to be a misunderstanding there have to be two of you, and what is a head-on collision if not a misunderstanding? Turnuspeed cut over the road to turn left then, seeing the grey Porsche arriving at tarmac level, decided to brake and stopped in roughly the middle of the road. It can be supposed that in his Porsche Jimmy hadn't braked and was waiting to see which way that damned Ford was going to go, so that he could go round it. But the chicane closed and the crash occurred.

In the next day's newspapers, Dean was obviously the one they called the bad driver. His reputation, his car, his destination; the fact that—that same morning, going through Bakersfield—he had been had up for exceeding the speed limit (70 mph [110 km/h] instead of the authorized 55 mph [90 km/h], nothing spectacular). It's not a question here of rehabilitating him by accusing his "rival," which was also done a bit later. Two contradictory sentences don't make a balanced one. But it has to be admitted that, by hesitating, Turnuspeed really did lay a trap for Dean. Dean might have avoided him had he had better reflexes. In any case, it's easier not to think that Dean's own clumsiness was responsible for his own death.

That was where Jimmy's life stopped and his legend, which was otherwise rich in twists and developments, started.

At the time of his death on September 30, 1955, Jimmy was not a great film star. The best-known thing he had done was a commercial for Pepsi. But *Rebel Without a Cause* came out in the week he died. Not only did Dean have the main part, once again a teenager with problems, but the scenario included a scene that would remain in people's minds. During a gathering of car-toting hoodlums, two of them defied each other; this had nothing to do with healthy rivalry, doing a gentle lap just to warm up the reflexes, but with a more primitive level of car sports. Two cars, side by side, raced towards a cliff: the one who jumped out of his car last would win. Nathalie Wood gave the start. The Mercury 49 and the Ford 48 sped along and Nicolas Ray, the producer, did not spare the viewers any of the atmosphere aboard the two vehicles. The swank who made the challenge in the first place lost his nerve first, in fact, but got the sleeve of his leather jacket caught in the door handle and, before he could work out how to break free, he took the great leap. Dean, in his little red nylon jacket, who had held out longest, had just enough time to roll out of his car and see both cars disappear into the night.

There was then an identity crisis that lasted a long time. *Rebel Without a Cause* is a psychological and sociological film, not an action film. But obviously the death of Jimmy Dean three days earlier in his car, wearing his character's famous red jacket, which he had adopted, provided a most appropriate background.

Jimmy's accident was one of those moments when cinema, that industry of emotion, was surpassed by this unexpected event, which was enough to trigger off a media maelstrom, in which journalists, essayists, and of course fans, began trampling each other underfoot and bellowing louder than each other, with sometimes a bit of real distress in the middle of the noise. The effect was extraordinary. The federal road safety services bought the wreck and exhibited it during a tour for educational purposes. The poor aluminum bodywork looked less like a car than sweet paper that had been crumpled up and thrown away in the gutter.

Then a stallholder bought the wreck and made people pay to sit in it, even though there was not much left. The rolling gear, which was still new, was removed for other Porsches (which met sticky ends, as the legend goes), and the precious engine with its four shafts was installed on a Lotus. The sale of posters must have generated more income than on any other film.

Frozen on the photos as an adolescent and at great speeds, James Dean will never get old.

Imagine Brando, forever slim, or Brad Pitt never becoming a father or meeting Angelina Jolie. James Dean has made the backstage more interesting than the canvas, with more realistic special effects.

He is probably the most famous accident victim, who earned a certain morbid and slightly crazy prominence that neither his actor's skill nor even the racing victories he dreamed of would have ever in reality have given him.

Driving or making films, exceptionally gifted and restless, James Dean had to do something with his life. Finally it was in his Porsche and by his death that he obtained the best screen presence.

1. Ronald Martinetti, *The James Dean Story: A Myth-Shattering Biography of an Icon*, Carol Publishing, 1996.

The white Porsche 356 Speedster, Dean's first racing car. He replaced it with the much more ambitious 550 Spyder.

Gianni (Giovanni) Agnelli
1921-2003

In Command

Dynasty, reign, power; these are the kind of regal words
that you have to use when speaking about Gianni Agnelli,
the Lord of Fiat and Prince of Italian Industry,
which he ran in his own way for more than thirty years.

Agnelli had that lightness, that elegance in everything that the filmmaker Visconti (cousin by marriage to the Agnelli family) portrayed in the character of Tancredo, in his film *The Leopard*. He was a haughty character with a superior mind, who had just enough humor to avoid the ridicule that a haughty person can attract. Only a few people knew him closely enough to have any other impression.

The first of the family tree was the grandfather, with the same first name (a practice which sets all the grand families apart), who took part in the foundation of FIAT (Fabbrica Italiana Automobili Torino) in 1899, then very quickly maneuvered so as to gain control himself, buying up shares when the company went public. There was a missing link: Giovanni's son, who disappeared in a floatplane accident. Gianni's mother, born a princess of Bourbon, was libertine and worldly, and died shortly after her husband disappeared. So Gianni spent his childhood under his grandfather's benevolent yoke, followed by law school. During the war he served in the armored corps first on the Russian front then in Tunisia, initially on the German side, then alongside the Allies after the collapse of the Italo-German alliance. And so here was Gianni, called *L'Avvocato*, the first male of the new generation and the heir at twenty-four to the Agnelli billions and the Fiat Empire, including

press, aviation, armaments, and several dozen car factories.

Did the young man have any business sense? He didn't have a taste for it, that's for sure. Leaving the giant company in the hands of a professor of economy, he preferred the aesthetic and sensual life of a young billionaire who liked skiing (his grandfather had founded a ski resort at Sestrières), art, football (the Turin club, Juventus, was his real passion), and fast driving. The word "playboy" seemed to have been coined specially for him, as he cruised on beautiful yachts from San Remo to Saint-Tropez, helming them himself, welcoming aboard the young Prince Rainier of Monaco as well as Errol Flynn or Porfirio Rubirosa.

One early morning in 1952, on the Côte d'Azur, his mistress, Pamela Churchill, surprised him in the company of the charming but somewhat young Anne-Marie d'Estainville (aged seventeen). Gianni was ordered to leave the villa with his companion, which he did at the wheel of his Ferrari, driving furiously. On the Cap Martin road, he ran very fast into a van, killing both its occupants; Anne-Marie was all right but Gianni was seriously injured. His right leg had to be amputated, which meant that he could no longer ride, but which did not prevent him for long from skiing, nor from leading the life he chose to lead.

Gianni Agnelli (facing
page) had the career
of an industrialist
and of a playboy, the life
of a potentate and
a dilettante; somewhere
between pleasure
and power—but taking
pleasure from the
power, too.

"Men can be divided in two categories, those who speak of women, and those who speak to women. Me? I prefer not to speak of them at all."

He had a reputation for amorous intrigue which was both constant and absent-minded, such as was attributed to Louis XIII, and which he kept up with biting aphorisms.

"Do I fall in love sometimes? After the age of twenty, only skivvies fall in love!"

Pamela Churchill got tired of him. Giovanni had been credited with a thousand affairs, especially with Anita Ekberg, the statuesque star of *La Dolce Vita*. But it was the elegant aristocrat Marella Caracciolo whom he eventually married.

In 1966 he took control of Fiat, with his taste for politics finally getting the better of pleasure. He already controlled the futures of all Italian car workers, together with those of the Russians and Poles working at Lada and Polski, and many South Americans by creating a lot of plants there. Agnelli was on first-name terms with the Kennedys, did business with Khrushchev and Gaddafi, ran Italy's foreign policy by himself; he also controlled its industry, defense, culture, social relations—not to mention sport. When you reign over so many men, you have to control their enthusiasms. Agnelli also set up and fostered the cult of Juventus, the Turin football club and soon-to-be star of Italian football. On the car side in 1969, Fiat bought up Ferrari and made it the standard-bearer for the whole of the Italian car industry. In fact Fiat entirely summed it up actually, since Agnelli had also bought himself Lancia, Alfa Romeo, and Maserati.

When you reign over the mass production of almost everyone's cars, you certainly don't go around driving just anything, nor do you buy anything other than what your group produces. Agnelli therefore ordered tailor-made cars, especially by Ferrari and Pininfarina, which was an elegant way of influencing the managers. The 365 "Triposto" (three seats) was the most famous of these "specials." At a time when the Commendatore Enzo Ferrari refused to use the mid-engined layout for his cars in the upper range (keeping it for the smaller and more affordable Dinos), Agnelli insisted on a big Ferrari designed his way, proving both that it was indeed possible, and that he was always above the underlings, including those of important people who bought

themselves production series Ferraris. In the meantime, the three-seater, with the driver's seat in the middle, enabled him to travel accompanied but without ever giving his passenger sweetheart the illusion of being the only and indispensable complement. Malicious gossip naturally talked of a more improper crew.

It must be rather a special feeling, which even few sovereigns have ever known, to read in your own morning newspapers the accounts of your own football team's match, the stock market quotations of your own companies, right up to accounts of your own escapades in the society pages.

L'Avvocato, suffering from cancer, died in 2003, but not before organizing who was to succeed him: one of his nephews, Gianni Elkann, enthroned at twenty-one, and thus recalling quite a few memories—an elegant way of approving his own personal destiny.

Agnelli was just as happy busying himself taking over Ferrari, in 1969, as he was launching the 500, the best-selling model that sold nearly 3,900,000 units.

Agnelli drove around in tailor-made Ferraris but he was also responsible for both much more modest and more ambitious cars: the Fiats, that put Italy and a fairly large proportion of the world

Françoise Sagan
1935-2004

An Internal Drive

Life, and fast. At the age when others read, Françoise Quoirez wrote. At eighteen, under the name of Sagan, she earned rapid success. With her first novel *Bonjour Tristesse*[1], she was immediately famous, bathed in a mix of admiration and scandal. We would be surprised nowadays by the boundless chorus of praise that proclaimed a natural genius, even at the risk of corrupting it.

It is also even more difficult to imagine all those other opinions, no doubt more numerous, voiced by the right sort of people who held their noses to pronounce against the very young girl. Such decadence; an anathema such that our age can no longer imagine. There was so much calm boldness in such a young girl, such a liberty of tone that she did not even take the trouble to put herself forward as a rebel, and some people could not accept that.

So Sagan, the public person, had been dealt with, couched in a controversy that now followed all her movements, her good books and her not so good ones, her plays and her film scripts, her parties and her loves. A paradoxical person had been born, a writer who was famous before she had built up her oeuvre; a young woman who had been pushed into the light of the flashbulbs, both a spoilt and a misunderstood child. Sagan, who was calmly amoral and rich, or at least living as though she was, became an object of pure scandal, just as much for the starchy bourgeoisie as for the left-wing fighters who were much listened to at the time.

Success, money, and immediately a car. First novel, first car, first Jaguar, an XK 140.

But this was neither a whim nor a pose: she really liked cars, particularly sports cars, English and soft-topped ones, ACs or Jaguars or Aston Martins. Perhaps it was because you are alone in them or accompanied only by those you want with you; and also because, when driving, Sagan very quickly found a source of sensuality and a stimulus for her imagination.

Cars and speed always took her far from where she was expected, and drew her further into her own sensitivity and finesse as a writer. The upmarket car fitted well into her type of life, so free. Reading her books, she tells us in so many accounts of this love of traveling, of speed, and of cars.

"My love of cars goes back to my childhood. I see myself at the age of eight sitting on my father's knees, "driving", holding the big black steering wheel."[2] You can pick this up in her novels, of course. In the description of a character, the way he or she drives defines them or summarizes their moods. The car is also used as an accessory in the story, a backdrop, the privileged place for emotions and encounters.

In her first novel, *Bonjour Tristesse*, she wrote: "She let me drive. At night the road

Françoise Sagan (facing page) and her perpetual rebelliousness embodied the modern young girl, scandalizing the Establishment.

appeared so beautiful that I drove slowly. Anne was silent; she did not even seem to notice the noisy radio. When my father's car passed us at a curve she remained unmoved. I felt I was out of the race, watching a performance in which I could not interfere." And, again, nearer the end of the novel: "Anne's car was made for sleeping. It rode so gently, not noisy like a motorcycle."[3]

Cars were made for cutting up the road but they also haunt the Parisian nights.

"My brother and I love driving at each other in our cars, at top speed, on the Place Saint-Sulpice, but we stop at six inches apart!"[4]

There was indeed something that could disturb the mainly pedestrian France of the time. Between Françoise and that brother of hers, Jacques Quoirez, the one-upmanship continued. In 1966 he ordered, or rather financed, a special car from the new company Lamborghini and the Carrozzeria Touring: the Flying Star coupé-break. Meanwhile, in 1957, Françoise ran into one of life's difficult moments. In her Aston Martin DB2, soft-top of course, it was always Françoise who drove. Usually a whole carload of young or future writers: Valdemar Lestienne, Berbard Franck, Veronique Campion. An

Her 1957 accident, at the wheel of this Aston Martin Cabriolet, almost cost her her life, and the result was an addiction to heroin that she never really overcame.

almost fatal accident occurred that challenged this marvelous insouciance, as some spiteful people—for whom this accident seemed a kind of vengeance—might say. Her passengers were safe and sound but not the driver: she had a fractured skull, crushed thorax, broken pelvis, and very almost died.

"I never take risks. I drive fast but carefully. It was a stupid accident. Five cars are known to have overturned at the same spot, three 4CVs and two Arondes. I wasn't in top gear so I couldn't go fast."[5]

When she was over her injuries, but certainly not her passion, she continued to drive exotic, shiny cars. In 1958 she visited Maranello, Enzo Ferrari's hunting ground, where there weren't yet any tourist coaches flocking at the gates. Always sensitive to young women and intrigued by her personality, the proud *Ingeniere* lent her a Spyder 250 GT California. In his own book, *My Terrible Joys*[6], Ferrari recalled the encounter. Considering the writer to be rather frail, he explained that the accident occurred because the car was too heavy for her: This was a rather strange theory, but not surprising coming from someone who was inclined to stigmatize woman's weakness. Whatever, Françoise still liked speed.

Who did she like? Nobody really knew, but as for cars, she loved them so much she gave them thoughts and feelings.

The prodigal child got old, of course, unless it was the world around her which was taking a brutal turn for youth! The events of May 1968 woke up Paris, exalted its disgust for political rigidity and its anticonformism, but there again the worldly character she had become accompanied her everywhere.

At the Odéon, revolutionaries shouted at her and accused her of coming to the

demonstrations in a Ferrari. How should she have replied? "No, it's a Maserati, and that changes everything." It's not certain if this argument was clear for those present but it was one way out, a snappy answer, as usual. And it was true that the high-powered cars built at the time by Maserati had, as far as the experts were concerned, a more intimate feel, more collusive engines and were suppler, less flamboyant, and less obsessed with high revs than the Ferraris. Sagan could have even mentioned still more exotic names.

A few years earlier, she had bought a prototype Gordini for herself, designed for Le Mans.

Amédée Gordini, known on the French circuits as the "Sorcier", (the 'Wizard"), had a workshop on Boulevard Victor, on the edge of the fourteenth arrondissement; it was a den, a craftsman's stall, which often echoed late into the night with the braying of eight cylinders inline being tuned, of metal being beaten by hand on the wooden templates to make that alloy of hope and state-of-the-art technology which becomes a racing car.

Skeptical by nature, Sagan nonetheless frequented the very society that she scorned.

121

The Jaguar XK 120 bought
with the royalties
of *Bonjour Tristesse*.
The Sagan legend had begun....

The factory, Gordini's den, not so far from the cellars of Saint-Germain, vibrated with another type of nightwalker. As she happened to wander around anonymously, during intimate intervals between fashionable places, Sagan must have stopped there and loved the old Wizard. One day he was, as usual, between fortune and bankruptcy (like her, actually) and she bought a racing car dating from the previous year to help him pay his bills for the future, next year's car. At the time, racing cars were registered; these weren't the type of cars to be put into just anybody's hands. This unreasonable car, this high-class racer, was the car that was capable of organizing everything for her, up there at around 150 mph (250 km/h), inside a sharp, inflexible cockpit, those face to faces with herself, that exaltation of mastery and fragility which is called speed.

Her age and her war wounds—a fractured pelvis that had become fragile again—had gradually deprived her of cars and almost of walking. But her son Denis would tell the story[7] of her last trip in a funny sort of car, a Smart Cabriolet, in which she showed none of the kind of gravity that serious literary figures might be expected to display; a way of cocking a snook, a joyous epitaph: *Bonjour Jeunesse*, "Good Morning Youth."

1. Éd. Julliard, 1954.

2. *Répliques*, éd. Quai Voltaire, 1992. (Our translation)

3. Françoise Sagan, *Bonjour Tristesse*, EP Dutton and Company, 1955. Translated by Irene Ash.

4. Interview in *Paris Match*. (Our translation)

5. Interview with *L'Express*, 1957. (Our translation)

6. Enzo Ferrari, *My Terrible Joys*, Hamish Hamilton Ltd., 1963.

7. *Paris Match*, September 29, 2004. (Our translation)

Juan Manuel Fangio
1911-1995

The Benchmark

Even today, any driver who thinks he's fast, hears the saying: "Who do you think you are?—Fangio?" Meaning: if you were Fangio, you'd be allowed to. Fangio was the myth, the supreme driver, the five-times champion, the driving ace.

First of all he had to invent driving for himself. Juan Manuel Fangio was born a long way from the racing circuits, in a small town in deepest Argentina, Balcarce, 250 miles (400 km) from Buenos Aires, 6,875 miles (11,000 km) from Monza. He was the fourth of six children. His parents were penniless Italian immigrants. School lasted only until he was eleven, then he worked in the forge at Balcarce, then of course in a garage.

He also had to invent, or almost, his first racing car: it was a Ford "Special," on which he had himself forged a lot of the parts. On the other hand there were roads there, but not nice smooth tracks, bordered with stands. In the South America of the Thirties, that of Fangio, the racing driver was still somewhat of a pioneer. There were some crude beaten-earth circuits but the big thing was the inter-town race, fought over with TCs—*turismo de competiciòn*. Fangio dared to set up his own business as a mechanic, and at night he did up his own car. The first *carreras—*races—in which he participated, took place along *carreteras*—earthen tracks, of course, not properly traced out, almost mobile. You had to *improvise* and then you had to hold out, and get the mechanics to hold out too. These were stages of ten or fifteen hours at full speed across the pampas, expecting a trap at any moment, then up into the mountains—and what mountains: the Cordillera of the Andes with its passes at over 13,000 feet (4,000 m). All this was interspersed with mechanical "games," with meager onboard means and rather primitive ingenuity. Later, the world champion, admiring the tremendous job done by the Marabello or Stuttgart mechanics, admitted to some other less orthodox "tricks," like making up for a lack of oil by adding water so that the crankshaft could at least bathe in the lubricant floating on the surface of this rather unconventional liquid.

Fangio made a local name for himself by winning some of these *carreras*, which occurred once or twice a year. It took time. When Fangio became famous throughout Argentina, he was already twenty-nine, and he had just beaten the great Oscar Galvez in the Gran Premio del Norte. Leaving Buenos Aires at midnight, 227 miles (363 km) towards Tucuman, then 402 miles (644 km) to La Quiaca and the highest plateaus of Bolivia, then 313 miles (501 km) to Potosi, then 327 miles (524 km) to La Paz, then 370 miles (592 km) to Arequipa along the Titicaca, then 400 miles (641 km) to Nazca and finally 312 miles (500 km) to Lima; and then all that was left to do was come back; in all eleven days and some 5,625 miles (9,000 km) of racing.

Luckily for him Argentina, was bubbling with excitement. Juan Perón, the recently elected president, wanted some champions

A helmet that would only protect you from flying stones; two pairs of goggles for the longest Grand Prix: truly this was the era of "shirtsleeves" racing.

and organized a season of international races, taking advantage of what was the winter break in Europe. The Simca-Gordini team, as always looking for bonus payments, was there; Amédée Gordini, the smart cookie, hired Fangio; he was a local hero and so it was one driver less to pay the fare for. Fangio turned out to be the equal of his teammate Jean-Pierre Wimille, at the time thought to be one of the world's best drivers. Sportingly, Wimille himself drew attention to this "local hope's" first-rate skills. Fangio had earned his place for Europe and, according to the second part of Perón's plan, flew Argentina's yellow and blue colors there. Nobody realized how high those colors were going to fly.

In 1949 Fangio devoted himself to the minor, but well-rewarded Grand Prix: San Remo, Pau, Perpignan, Marseilles—and won them all! This unknown driver, who did not always have the best cars, outdrove everyone from Prince Bira to Baron de Graffenried. Naturally his successes, and especially the way in which he acquired them (apparently effortlessly), began to build him a reputation. One German journalist wrote: "Fangio is so calm that you'd think he was asleep!" His face was impassive and he barely moved. While other drivers gesticulated with the big steering wheels when going round a bend, Fangio did it all with one deft movement, in one direction, and faster than everybody else.

Physically Fangio was rather ordinary. A bit on the chubby side, with not much hair and with crooked legs, Fangio's nickname El Chueco, "the bow-legged one," stuck with him. It was a defect which reminded the South American journalists of the gauchos of the Argentinean pampas! But his arms were powerful. His voice was surprisingly high-pitched but controlled: Fangio expressed himself methodically like a timid person who is forced to speak. He always wore very simple racing gear, without any affectation or distinctive feature: mechanics' trousers and a simple polo shirt. Backstage there were never any scenes. Fangio was accompanied everywhere by Beba, like him from Balcarce, whom some took for his watchful wife, although they never married. Later, he regretted not having had a family. His offbeat career would no doubt not have helped. But how do you explain Fangio's prestige and the fascination he caused? Together with his results and his driving, whose panache, safety, and superiority contrasted with the man's discretion, Fangio had a particular look. His very light blue eyes were intense, as if he was staring at a point on the inside of the track. Cars in those days were cut away a lot, enabling everybody to see the driver's calm movements. His goggles hid nothing of that tense, keen look.

The Mercedes W196 gave Fangio two of his five world championship titles, in 1954 and 1955.

The drivers' World Championships started the following year in 1950. Varzi and Wimille were killed shortly before them. Meanwhile Count Trossi died of illness, and the bosses at Alfa hesitated over which drivers to choose. They finally gave Fangio his opportunity, since so many people were saying how good he was. Juan Manuel won three races out of six: Monaco, Spa, Rheims. This was the beginning of an exceptional cycle. Out of the fifty-one Grand Prix he took part in, he won twenty-four, a record which is still unbeaten; and five World Formula 1 titles out of the eight he took part in, for Alfa Romeo, Maserati, Ferrari, Mercedes, and then Maserati again. The number of times he could have been beaten driving equivalent cars could be counted on the fingers of one hand.

Moss managed once to outdo the man he himself called "Maestro." In the very trying 1955 Mille Miglia, he did the 1,000 miles (1,600 km) at an average speed of 99.375 mph (159 km/h). Fangio was miles behind. Defeated? In fact, for the first time Moss had had recourse to a navigator, the journalist Denis Jenkinson who, using a series of arm movements, announced the way the road was going, bend after bend, by reading the notes they had taken on a recce earlier from a scroll. Fangio drove alone; ever since that day in Argentina in 1948 when he fell into a ravine with his friend Daniel Urrutia, he refused to have a co-driver. He alone had survived the crash and he had always felt responsible for his friend's death.

Fangio had another accident, at Monza in 1952. He had raced in Ireland on Saturday, gone to Lyon by plane, then finished the trip by car to Monza just in time to take a shower. He had then settled himself into his Maserati at the back of the grid—as he hadn't taken part in the trials— and started to make his way back to the front of the group. Was it presumptuous of him? Had tiredness clouded his legendary judgment? This time, Fangio hit the barrier marking out the inside lane; he took off and broke his cervical vertebrae. A priest was called and he was given Extreme Unction, he was saved, just: end of season. "I saw how easy it was to go over from life to death, practically without realizing it."

But at a time when every race was marred by a tragedy, Fangio escaped accident so often that it fed his legend.

Thus, in 1950 at Monaco, before the end of the first lap, Nino Farina's Alfa, which had slewed across the track, was hit by nine cars which had crashed into the unseen obstacle one by one. Fangio was in the lead and arrived at top speed but slowed down at the last moment *before* coming upon and seeing the accident. He avoided his rivals' wrecks, passed through, and won the race. He kept the explanation for this miracle to himself for a very long time, but did eventually divulge that as he was finishing the first lap in the lead, he saw that the spectators weren't looking at him, and supposed

that something had happened just after the bend, by then behind him. This intuition was remarkable, proof that the champion's field of vision, his acuity, was above normal.

Almost the same scenario was repeated in 1955 in dramatic circumstances during the Le Mans accident. Fangio was chasing Mike Hawthorn's Jaguar right from the beginning. The two men overtook each other several times, beat the lap records and beat them again, lapped the laggards over and over again. At 18.27, they came into sight again of the stands at more than

The British Grand Prix, Aintree, 1955: Fangio (No. 10), between his teammate, Stirling Moss (No. 12) and Jean Behra's Maserati. Three hours 7 minutes and 21 seconds later, Moss won in front of his home crowd. He never knew whether or not Fangio, two-tenths of a second behind him, had let him win.

Monaco, 1955: "Nobody knew how
to take bends like [Fangio] did,"
Denis Jenkinson, the
automobile journalist
and Stirling Moss's navigator.

175 mph (280 km/h). They caught up with the Mercedes driven by Fangio's stable-mate, the Frenchman, Levegh, who along this straight line was only just slower than them. These three cars also overtook a slow Austin Healey on the right of the track. Suddenly Hawthorn veered off to the right and slammed his brakes on: he no doubt wanted to waste as little time as possible on his refueling stop. The surprised Healey driver swung away, cutting Levegh's path; the two cars touched each other; the Mercedes took off and the Healey spun round. Fangio passed practically underneath the flying Mercedes and continued on his way, leaving behind him what was one of the most tragic accidents that had ever occurred in car racing: Levegh's Mercedes exploded among the crowd, killing eighty-two people and the driver.

Later that night, Mercedes withdrew from the race as a sign of mourning. Fangio won the Le Mans 24 Hours, which he never entered again. International public opinion rose against the races, against the organizers, against Mercedes, against the drivers. When Hawthorn, Macklin, and especially Levegh were all hysterically called into question, Fangio's skill served as proof, as a counter-example. At the time he was already a legend. He was already twice World Champion and was once again in the lead in the Grand Prix season. Fangio was content to bear witness to the fact that on the contrary it was Levegh who had saved him: several seconds before the crash he had raised his hand to signal he was overtaking the Healey.

The third miracle was a bit different. During his last season, in 1958, he was invited to take part in the Cuba Grand Prix, organized by the dictator Batista to boost his own standing. Fangio found he was trapped: he was given a bad car, nice and shiny but with a twisted chassis and the circuit which used the Malecón, the Havana sea front, was dangerous, and badly set out. He was worried, but the evening before the Grand Prix, he was kidnapped at gunpoint by a group of Castro's rebels and held for the duration of the race, to sabotage the event, embarrass Batista, and draw international attention to the country. The race nonetheless took place and ended in a massacre: a car left the track, crashing into the crowd and killing six. The race finished in such chaos that the drivers decided to share out the prize money equally.

Fangio returned to South America to take part in the Carrera Pan-Americana with his keenest rivals. To put your foot down on Mexico's earth roads, to get the Lancia's engine to sing out between Tuxtla and Oaxaca, to record better averages than 125 mph (200 km/h), with peaks at 162.5 mph (260 km/h), you need something just a bit more than a sportsman's simple vanity. To the horse-drawn carts and falling stones add narrow tires, which were just waiting to burst, and which did burst, dragging the impudent and reckless driver into swirls of red metal and dust. They came out of it all sheepish and bruised, with tanned leather and emotions, ready for other escapades; or they didn't come out of it at all; for many of them disappeared, carried away because they lost control or because of some mechanical failure. But Fangio, he got through. And it was of his own free will that he put an end to his racing. It had been a flamboyant career, running across embers during the most dangerous, deadliest period in car racing history. His last Grand Prix was again marred by the death of a first-class driver, Luigi Musso.

What is it that makes a driver's glory? First his results and the way they are acquired; then the public's affection, and the respect of his peers. Fangio, El Chueco, finally withdrew with an unequalled score, an unequalled respect among the other drivers, and a reputation that was so well founded that it is still here today, half a century after his last race. And his rivals never had a word to say against him, nor did they ever reproach him for dangerous tactics.

Naturally Fangio's financial situation benefited from his "European Campaign." After a dozen top-level races, Juan Manuel became a rich man, but it was a fortune that doesn't bear any relation to that of today's sporting stars. His father, the mason, built his son's beautiful house himself, in Balcarce, obviously. And Juan Manuel never stopped working, running a Mercedes agency and accepting the role as the make's ambassador.

The firm's serious chairman nonetheless admitted that, in his hands, the make's staid limousines did move along the pampas roads at unusual speeds.

Enzo Ferrari

1898-1988

A Leader of Men

A talented driver, Enzo Ferrari became a household name by managing engineers and drivers, first for Alfa Romeo, then with his own racing team, Scuderia Ferrari.

The factory that Enzo Ferrari set up at Maranello in the Modena suburbs has become a place of international pilgrimage for fans of this man. What right have we to meddle with this iconic image? Having left the army after the end of the war, Enzo Ferrari began as a test driver for Vespa, then worked as a racing driver. He distinguished himself especially with CMN (Costruzioni Meccaniche Nazionali) then with Alfa Romeo. Although he was quite good, on his own admission he was not as good as the aces of the day. He was as proud as a driver can be, but he was also sufficiently intelligent to realize that he would not succeed in gaining the power and money to which he aspired by remaining behind the steering wheel. He took a step back to consider the racing world as a whole.

There were automobile companies that had to make themselves known and get their products appreciated, actor-drivers who were running after a fee, organizers who wanted to present the most beautiful cars to a public that was ready to pay, a press corps that accompanied and amplified the spectators' adulation for the great racing personalities and the most successful cars. He recognized that there was something missing in this set-up: someone who could organize the relations between the drivers and the carmakers, who could manage the former for the benefit of the latter, who would be able to negotiate their presence with the organizers, and who would know how to get the press to give an advantageous description of the exploits accomplished.

In 1929 he founded the Scuderia (Italian for "stable") that bore his name. Although other drivers had tried to establish this sort of set-up (including Tazio Nuvolari and Emilio Materassi), these had been above all to help their own careers, and they had only succeeded moderately. Ferrari imposed himself quickly by the quality of his organization. The Scuderia needed a coat of arms: it chose those of the Italian aviator Francesco Baracca, a friend of Gabriele d'Annuncio, who had been shot down in 1918 after scoring thirty-four kills. One evening, after Enzo had won a race, the hero's mother agreed to let Enzo use them on his car. The rearing horse on a golden background never left him. As the story goes, it came from the coat of arms of the town of Stuttgart; Baracca had adopted it after shooting down a German pilot from that town. And it's the same emblem, though smaller, which appears on Porsche's insignia.

Scuderia Ferrari raced Maseratis, Duesenbergs and even motorbikes, but above all Alfa Romeos. So much so that, after a few seasons, it officially represented the Milanese company. Although he did not take his studies any further, despite his father's wishes, Enzo Ferrari was sufficiently knowledgeable about technical matters to choose the best from among the drivers and the engineers. He exercised his influence right into the design offices, in keeping both with his racing successes and with the kind of addiction to the very beautiful

People remember an old man in a press conference who commented on the triumphs of his Scuderia as if they were the finances of a kingdom. But Enzo Ferrari had also been a driver (facing page).

His cars raced everywhere and won ... almost everywhere. Here, at Indianapolis in 1952, Alberto Ascari had to abandon the race after forty laps.

cars that any Italian engineer might have. More particularly, it was he who stole the great Vittorio Jano, designer of the superb Alfa Romeo P2, 6C, 8C 2300, and 158 Alfetta, away from Fiat. It is fair to say that there was a part of Enzo Ferrari in these very great cars.

But within his own company he struggled to exert influence. A rival of Spanish origin, Wilfredo Ricart, the future designer of the Pegaso cars, worked—according to Ferrari—to discredit him with the management at Alfa Romeo. In 1939, Ferrari left the company. In rather a paradoxical way, the company recognized his worth by forbidding him contractually to use his own name for four years. That is why the very first "Ferrari," of which three examples were built, was called Auto Avio Costruzioni 815. Two 815s took part in the Mille Miglia in 1940, dominating the race in their category before breaking down because of small mechanical problems. But once the turmoil of war had passed by, Ferrari could at last return to constructing under his real name. In 1947 he presented a little runabout fitted with a surprising 1,500 cc V12 engine. Success wasn't long in coming. It was the first of a really long list of triumphs.

After all the bloodletting of its double war, first alongside Hitler's armies and then the Allies', Italy dreamed of triumphing again with the image of this red car making its way through the crowds gathered together at the gates.

From then on, Enzo Ferrari became the ruler of his domain at Maranello (a domain which actually belonged to his wife). There, racing cars were built which were sent to the four corners of

the world to earn the starting fees and victories which were their *raison d'être*. The best drivers in the world were honored to drive for him. It was there also that the excessively expensive road versions were built, which Ferrari considered a secondary source of revenue. His customers were Leopold of Belgium, Gianni Agnelli, and Ingrid Bergman. He ruled over high society's desires; he dominated the aristocrats as well as the great artists.

He became known as Commendatore, an unofficial title with which all captains of industry are politely honored in Italy. He preferred *"Ingeniere"* (Engineer), which he obtained much later as an honorary title from the University of Bologna. Ferrari reigned. His life could now merge with his cars' increasing success. However, sadly this success was marred by tragedy: Dino, his dear son and a gifted engineer, who had a promising career ahead of him, died in 1956 from muscular dystrophy. Devastated, Ferrari always wore dark glasses in public after then. And at the same time, after the victories came the accidents and all the controversy: the involvement of a Ferrari in the terrible Mille Miglia accident of 1957 led to his indictment but subsequent acquittal on manslaughter charges. Each time one of his cars was involved in a fatal motor racing accident, the press attacked him vigorously. Ferrari, who read the Italian and international press every morning, and who had even imagined he could become a sports columnist, was very much affected by these attacks. He became less accessible. In 1969, he reached an agreement with Fiat, the giant Italian company at which he had tried getting a job in 1918. Fiat now owned a stake in his business, freeing him from ultimate responsibility His success was complete. Enzo Ferrari could work from one day to another running the racing section like a small production series car department. A second son, Piero Lardi-Ferrari, was born from a second relationship that remained secret until the death of Enzo's legitimate wife; he is at present the firm's vice chairman. And what about the drivers? Their relations with the great man were stormy and heated.

It is difficult nowadays to hint at there being any darker side where this legendary figure is concerned. But his drivers knew about his taste for psychological intrigues, and mocked him for it. Among themselves they called him Al Capone. Olivier Gendebien also blamed him several times for setting one driver against another. According to Gendebien, several days before the Mille Miglia that was to have been the main event of the 1957 season, Ferrari had "motivated" them. "You Gendebien you take the GT and you Portago you take the Sport and I'll be surprised if you go faster than he does." For a driver this was more than just incitement, it was a challenge—or even an ultimatum—and in the end Portago died . The other drivers were also "motivated" in the same manner. For example, if he won, Peter Collins, the Maranello favorite, had been promised a Gran Turismo, whereas his co-driver—the journalist Klemantaski—was counting on winning enough to be able to afford an Alfa Julietta. Enzo led

his men like an officer leads his, knowing that in building up the red legend and the company, his racing stable, there would almost inevitably be losses, just as an officer expects losses in war. This cynicism—or at least a certain detachment— was an integral part of his job.

Nonetheless, apart from admiring them with his expert eye, Ferrari admitted to having a really soft spot for some of the most colorful and the most committed drivers. First the young French hope, Guy Moll, before the war. Then in the Fifties Peter Collins, who lived in the white house with red shutters at Fiorano, Enzo's own house in the heart of what—years later, in 1972—was to be the first private circuit for a Formula 1 stable. Finally Gilles Villeneuve, the Quebecois tightrope walker. All three of them were killed driving cars bearing his colors. Enzo Ferrari's refusal to be present at the competitions has been attributed to his haughty character, but mightn't it rather have been that mixture of enthusiasm and pain that attached him to racing forever. Mightn't it rather have been what he called his "terrible joys."[1]

1. Enzo Ferrari, *My Terrible Joys*, Hamish Hamilton Ltd., 1963.

Maranello, 1961. Each year, Ferrari presented his new models to the press: here the F1 156 and the 246 P. After for a long time proclaiming that "horses did not push the cart," he eventually gave in to the British idea of the rear engine.

The Sixties and Seventies

The Golden Age

So, driving for the masses had been achieved. The man in the street had a car; it had become a symbol, both coveted and contested, of modernity. But having a car was no longer enough: now you had to make an informed choice about which model. The car changed town living as much as it did the countryside; it dominated industry, and stimulated banking. Passions were exacerbated and diversified. In order to assert that they were a better than average driver, some people pushed themselves to the limits, whilst the racing drivers found themselves faced with machines that were ever more perfect, but also ever more demanding and dangerous.

Pat Moss
Soïchiro Honda
Claude Lelouch
Jean-Pierre Beltoise
Jean Rédélé
Jim Clark
Colin Chapman
Jackie Stewart
Pierre Bardinon
Johnny Servoz-Gavin
Brock Yates
Gilles Villeneuve
Steve McQueen
Jean-Claude Andruet
Graham Hill

Pat Moss
1934-2008

On the Roundabout

At eight, Patricia Moss won a riding competition—
on a pony. Then she moved on to horses and then cars.
A desire for movement, a love of speed.

Some men are the first to deplore the fact that racing cars is a man's sport. When by some quirk of fate a girl is really interested in cars, she is accepted rather well. Naturally if she turns out to be among the best of the racing drivers and starts to challenge male supremacy, things aren't so rosy. Apart from stupid remarks, tougher reactions cannot to be excluded. On the other hand, as far as sponsors are concerned, a girl taking up car racing is always a good story. But it's true that a driver's career is often marked by alternating ups and downs, and being a woman racing driver just makes things harder.

As for Pat Moss, she didn't need anybody. Did her older brother Stirling pass on some of his driver's secrets to her? Or it could have been their father, Alfred; by profession, he was a dentist, but Brooklands was a favorite haunt of his and his career as an enlightened amateur had taken him as far as the 1924 Indianapolis 500, where he finished with a respectable sixteenth place. Their mother had also tried doing some handling tests. It was maybe a matter of genes or family atmosphere, but the gracious Pat was definitely fast.

Accustomed to tough competition conditions as a memeber of the national horse-riding team, Pat took part in her first rallies in 1953 as a co-driver. After that she considered herself ready to take the wheel, and her first results, together with the family name (at the time Stirling was a Formula 1 racing

and endurance star), got her a car with Austin-Morris. She preferred the rallies: in 1958, she finished fourth in the very prestigious and demanding RAC rally, but she still didn't know what to do with her career. This was best demonstrated by the fact that, instead of the "civilian" car stipulated in the BMC contract, she asked for a van for carrying her horses! She won the Tulip Rally driving a Mini and, above all, the Liège–Rome–Liège marathon, driving a rough Austin Healey 3000, an easy stroll of a drive that involved crossing the Alps across the passes on unmetalled roads! It was the first victory in the overall classification to be achieved by a woman in an international competition. It would be tedious to list all her victories in women's competitions, but she was European champion five times. But above all she won a host of good results in the mixed classification, including three victories and seven podiums.

Unsurprisingly, such an intrepid young woman was enough to get all the racing drivers' rev counters jumping into the red. Pat was attracted to one of the best, the Swedish giant Eric Carlsson, whom she married in 1963. When chasing certain girls you have to be quick! She was then taken on by the Saab team. The same year she came third in the Monte Carlo rally! This earned her other contracts with Lancia (second at San Remo), then with Alpine, and finally with Toyota, and a career lasting twenty years.

The start of the 1964
Le Mans 24 Hours race
(p. 134).

Stirling Moss was one of
the greatest Grand Prix
divers. His young sister,
Pat, preferred rallies
(facing page). Their
mother and father
also raced.

Soïchiro Honda

1906-1991

Motorized Escape

Between Port Arthur (Japan's victory over Russia in 1905) and MacArthur (the American general who governed Japan after 1945), Honda grew up in a complex and troubled world, knocked about as everywhere else had been by the changes in new technology, but where the past, perhaps because it was richer, seemed harder to alter than it did elsewhere.

In Japan, the carp is said to possess sacred qualities, and it exists in all sorts of colors except blue. So, one could say that little Soïchiro—thanks to scientific curiosity and incorrigible insolence—succeeded in painting the venerable fish blue.

Soïchiro Honda was born in 1906. The mikado (the local emperor) nurtured great expansionist ambitions, encouraged by the successful national industrial advances that had been made in the navy, armor, and aviation. But, technologically and religiously, the countryside was still rooted in the Middle Ages. Little Soïchiro was the son of an ironsmith in Hamamatsu, 100 miles (160 km) from Tokyo and by this time overwhelmed by the Japanese megapolis. Brought up in a free environment, he turned out to be allergic to school, but fascinated by his father's forge, where he spent hours on end. It was in the village that he saw his first car. "The Ford had stopped in front of the most beautiful house with a noise of automated hell. Oil seeped from it, leaving a little puddle. It left just as quickly, as if to escape our curiosity or dispel our wonder. I had had the time to walk round it and admire it. But the driver who was watching over it prevented me from getting nearer; like a bonze or a temple guard he took great care of his divinity."[1]

For Soïchiro the West was just as mysterious and mythical as Asia could be in the mind of a Western schoolchild, but with a few surprises: he idolized Napoleon Bonaparte. No doubt the extent of the Frenchman's empire and his little size seemed to correspond to his own ambitions as much as it did to his own physique. Small and scrawny, Honda admitted that he did suffer from feeling inferior about this, but thought it might have been the reason for the energy he put into fitting an engine onto a motorcycle. When very young, he had become familiar with machines: first of all the steam de-husking machine that improved life in the paddy fields; then anything that moved.

"At my request, my father took me to the station to see the locomotives. The footplatemen were shoveling in huge quantities of coal. This operation avenged all my fears of hell. These machines were more powerful than the cauldrons I'd been threatened with and they'd been created by men."

The natural course was for him to become an apprentice in a Tokyo garage, where he received a very peculiar baptism in driving. On September 1, 1923, a terrible earthquake struck the town, causing thousands of deaths; during the first trembles, the boss shouted to the workers to

Soïchiro Honda stood alone as the embodiment of the "yellow peril" threatening Western industrial interests (facing page). Pragmatic? He most certainly was, but his success relied on his enthusiasm.

save the cars. Soïchiro managed to drive one and take a whole load of refugees to safety, several miles from the town. It was an extraordinary test of maturity: being able to overcome his panic in the middle of apocalypse when law and order collapsed with the rest.

Very keen on the technical side of his work, and delighted when he contributed something original, Honda also very quickly learned to like driving. In his little garage he experimented seriously (and patented a cast alloy wheel in 1931 at twenty-five), but more especially for his own use he built some very basic racers using big, stripped-down Fords. It was with one of these that regularly, as a winner, he advertised as a mechanic. He also went through the pains of a serious accident, when he crashed violently into a spectator's car, which had ventured onto the autodrome. His face remained partially paralyzed and his career as a driver was finished. But he remained reckless and fond of extreme forms of piloting—planes, cars, and motorbikes of all sorts.

In 1949, he took up the challenge and founded his own company, though at first it was only concerned with bicycles on which he fixed a generator engine. He rapidly designed a proper motorcycle, which was very successful commercially, the equivalent of the Vespa in Italy. Rather sneakily, Soïchiro admitted many years later that the frames on the first examples bent with the heat from the engine. The firm, which he wanted to be as lively as him, improved its products and continuously diversified. As early as 1955, he was number one in Japan. But that wasn't enough for him. Within his company, Soïchiro Honda was a warm, spontaneous, albeit sometimes patronizing, character, who could also be exacting, which made him a formidable jack of all trades, capable of mixing as easily with the research office staff, as with the assembly lines personnel or the cleaning teams. All the employees, whatever their position, wore white and donned a Honda cap, beginning with Soïchiro Honda himself, of course. In private Honda was a family man (his son Hirotoshi became an engineer), who did not forget to commit certain misdemeanors which another culture would consider serious, like making excessive "offerings" to the gods in the company of lovely geishas!

This caricature of the self-made man soon fed American and European journals with the old myth of the "yellow peril." As early as 1959, Honda decided to compete with the established market brands, and on terrain that was their pride: racing.

His objective was far from modest: to win the most famous competitions, and in less than three years. His machines took part and reached their objective; in the 1961 Tourist Trophy, five Hondas beat all the English and Italian machines. One hundred thousand Hondas were sold in a month; imagine how happily the other manufacturers welcomed Honda's entry into the car market! Certain people, in Turin, Longbridge, or Billancourt, hoped that the Japanese state would insist on that cap-wearing troublemaker doing what he was told. Indeed, at the time the Japanese state was very much in favor of a planned economy and hadn't envisaged a new company coming and upsetting the established order, Toyota and Nissan especially. But Honda insisted, overstepped and bypassed the restrictions, and was successful, using the same weapons as with his motorbikes—originality, smallness, and high technology—with racing at the highest level as the means of conveying its image and internal motivation. It was less easy, however, for four wheels than it was for two, because its rivals were more powerful, the customers less reactive, and the apprenticeship longer in Formula 1.

A more reasonable approach was needed—that of the ecological and reassuring Civic—to transform the bridgehead into a solid presence on the market. But this happened without Soïchiro; he had dreamed of the Civic as something light, miniature, and very simple: air-cooled and therefore rid of radiators, piping, and water pumps, but also noisier and more polluting. This detail was the point of no return with his board of directors, where for the first time his stubbornness did him no good. Disowned, he was "sacked" and moved sideways to the position of honorary chairman, and very well-paid shareholder. From then on the Hondas were no longer quite his cars; his name continued to build up his fortune, but no longer directly nourished his life. He was not even fifty-five and already his career was behind him. All the more so as the Civic, which he hadn't wanted, and which he certainly hadn't wanted in its present form, was a triumph everywhere. All that Soïchiro had left was racing: an incredible series of world titles with his motorbikes and, after 1984, in Formula 1, too. He also had his son's glory and success in a small motorbike racing firm, Mugen, attached to the giant Honda Motors but independent nonetheless. And finally, too, he could enjoy writing his memoirs and his memories of fishing blue carps.

Without a very serious accident that left him with half his face paralyzed, Soïchiro would most certainly have put all his energy into driving and not into industry.

1973, Soïchiro Honda next to Takeo Fujisawa, the vice-president of the brand (facing page top).

Soïchiro Honda in front of the first prototype F1 car on the sixtieth anniversary of Honda (facing page bottom).

1. Honda, Soïchiro, with Thierry de Beaucé and Christian Polak. *Honda par Honda*. Paris: Stock éditions, 1979.

Claude Lelouch
(b. 1937)

Private Showing

Have a good look. In almost all Claude Lelouch's films there is a car that helps to portray one of the characters or has a symbolic value. His films use cars to project ideas and emotions.

In *Un homme et une femme*, Jean-Louis Trintignant plays a racing driver. In *Il y a des jours ... et des Lunes*, Gérard Lanvin steals an Alpine. In *Les Uns et les Autres*, Francis Huster explains to high school pupils that speed radars do not work above 144 mph (230 km/h). In *Viva la vie*, a strange Lancia B 37 surrounds Michel Piccoli with an air of mystery. In *Les bons et les méchants*, Jacques Dutronc shows Jacques Villeret how well a Traction holds the road and immediately finds himself in a ditch. To write such scenes, you have to be someone who loves cars: they have to amuse, move, and attract you. Remember Trintignant, who had just won the Monte Carlo rally, receiving Anouk Aimée's telegram ("I love you") during the after-race banquet. He took his leave, disappeared, and set off again driving the Mustang that had just won the race. This trip from one end of France to the other, a postlude to the rally and a prelude to love, was as if suspended in time, during which the man, driving as fast as he could, was happy, thoughtful, and dreaming: in love.

The mad race in the opening minutes of *Vingt ans après* was an allegory of crossed destinies, determined struggles. Was the parable crystal clear? Was the effect successful or was it irrelevant? At any rate it was a high point in the art of filming realistic stunt driving.

In Lelouch's films, cars are important. Obviously not everybody likes his films. After a fifty-year career, more than forty-five films and

just as much dissension, what is never contested is the way he manages his actors, nor the way he uses his camera. "Driving and cinema writing are similar. I think that a good producer 'drives' his film. For me a close-up shot is like accelerating, a wide-angled shot is like braking." In addition to his real talent he really understands the place cars have in the lives of those who love them.

His father owned a Citroën Traction. It was after the war; peace had returned and the already old Traction regularly took the Lelouch family from Paris to Deauville. It was pampered, so much so that it had been fitted with a special radiator grill, like lots of accessory makers used to make, just to pander to their customers' taste for customization (for the amateurs they were called Tonneline, Langenthal, E.T., Robri, etc.).

At about the same time—he was ten—the man with the Traction offered Claude his first camera. This Kodak was also exactly ten years old, since it had been bought to film his birth. In short, as the son of a man who loved cars, Claude Lelouch was almost unavoidably among those who could enthuse about grease, oil, and dirt. And this can be seen in his films.

Lelouch, a self-styled dunce, planned his climb up the social ladder hanging on to his camera. He was a big director of Scopitone pictures, the ancestors of the film clip, cheaply made to be shown on those juke boxes fitted with

A camera is used to give movement to photography and is a natural ally of the car. Here, Claude Lelouch lies on the bonnet of a Ford Mustang in *Un homme et une femme* (facing page).

screens. "I worked for Gérard Sire who did not pay me. He owed me fifty thousand francs [in 1964 or 1965, this was a tidy sum] and he bought himself a magnificent, aubergine-colored Mercedes 280 SL, the cabriolet with the pagoda-shaped hardtop. I was not really angry, but I just drew his attention to the fact. So he just handed me the keys there and then. I didn't even have enough money to fill the tank. Obviously I wanted to sell it, but for several days, I couldn't leave it, it had become my office. And then I noticed that it was reassuring all my financiers. Besides it was at that time that I was able to sort out *Un homme et une femme* which up until then hadn't been making much headway." This was a nice confession. A lot is often said about how much a car costs, but never very much about what it can give its owner.

The shooting of *Rendez-vous* must not be forgotten. This one-reeler was at once surrounded by all sorts of stories. It was made in 1976, lasted 8 minutes and 39 seconds and was the sort of film that prevents all those who worry about cars from sleeping, and has been shown constantly on the blogosphere ever since it came out. Having a nine- or ten-minute reel to spare, Lelouch set out to make a sequence shot of crossing Paris as fast as possible one summer's morning, without any cutting, any editing. "Alone aboard my Mercedes 6.9 with the camera fixed to the bumpers, I crossed Paris at full speed. I passed the Etoile, the Champs-Elysées, the river banks, until I reached Montmartre, where a girl was waiting for the driver. There were people with walkie-talkies on the route but there was only one place that was really dangerous, without any visibility, and that was at the entrance to the Louvre which, at the time, used to be taken in the opposite direction, so that you'd come out at right angles to the Rue de Rivoli. I only found out afterwards that the walkie-talkie at that spot had not been working!" You gambler, you!

It was Jean-Louis Trintignant, the nephew of a great driver (Maurice) who suggested Lelouch make his character a racing driver in *Un homme et une femme*.

Stills from *Édith et Marcel*, 1983 (top) and *Les Bons et les Méchants*, 1975 (above).

Jean-Pierre Beltoise

(b. 1937)

Unbridled

The trick is to be born with a gift: to be born with the gift of driving in the Forties in France, and the firm belief that you're a champion, even though you are a million miles away from the garages, the money, the circuits.

It was with the Rosengart belonging to his father's butcher's shop that Jean-Pierre improved his driving skills. So here we had the Rosengart LR van, throwing its cargo around as it hurtled round bends while the novice butcher went through his driving apprenticeship. But before that there was the bike, and already the kids competed for the best times, and already there was a desire to be first. Jean-Pierre didn't particularly have a winner's build; although he was handsome he was more scrawny, which at first was an advantage for a driver, above all on the small motorbikes at the beginning of his career. Jean-Pierre had an absolute weapon, though: total determination; he would be number one. "It was quite crazy. It was more than ambition, it was madness."[1]

Jean-Pierre faked his papers to be able to pass his license a year before the legal age of seventeen; Jean-Pierre took part in races, Jean-Pierre won. The racing world noticed his talent, just like in his dream. Paco Bulto, founder of the Bultaco manufacturer, called him and offered him a Bultaco 125 for one round of the World Championships, at Imola. Jean-Pierre Beltoise was in the lead from the first lap. And the first time he braked heavily, three other bikes finally overtook him; three hardened riders, among whom were the legendary Mike Hailwood. It was only at that moment that Beltoise would admit that he was not alone on the track and that he had to reckon with his rivals.

That being said, he went on to win eleven French championship titles. The other bikers didn't think very much of Beltoise, however, because for him two wheels were only a springboard towards cars, which were his real dream.

The period, politics, which he found so uninteresting, impinged on him directly. "That b… Algerian War, where I almost deserted by crossing through a minefield at night, I had such a grudge against life, against everybody." He spent twenty-six months raging, while in the distance, in other theaters of operations, the real stakes, the real battles were being fought. In military times, the heroism of a Beltoise isn't worth very much; it is only sensitive to its own crusades.

When he got back to France, he returned to riding motorbikes, but accepted an apprenticeship (another one) with René Bonnet, a small-scale constructor who earned a living from doing up Panhard and Renault specials. But Beltoise was reduced to doing little jobs—in charge of oil changes during the week and racing motorbikes brilliantly at weekends. But even success and honors in the two-wheel field did not turn him away from his long-standing objective: car racing.

Months later, pressured by his nephew Georges, Bonnet agreed to try out "the champion." At the 1963 Le Mans he was awarded the Index of Performance, an award coveted by the constructors. This was one step

What's the point of knowing you're fast if you don't get the opportunity to race? Fortunately the fervent Jean-Pierre Beltoise (facing page) teamed up with Jean-Luc Lagardère and his Matra venture.

on the road, even though for him, a racing driver, Le Mans was not especially interesting. But this proof of his reliability enabled him to sign up for the small Formula 3 single-seaters for the 1964 season. This was his real chance. Even in an inferior machine, he immediately demonstrated a talent that suggested he was far from being a debutant—even though he was just that. That was fortunate, since he was already twenty-seven. Did he have the will to pull out all the stops? During the Rheims 12 Hours, a fast race if ever there was one, the frail René-Bonnet left the track, throwing him out; Beltoise endured an eight-day coma followed by ten months in bed.

It was one of those periods that brands you, bends your will, forces you to fight other fights; leads to re-education, recovery. But here again, a racing driver will recognize himself; his first, his only aim is to resume racing, to pick up the thread of the race and not "to waste the season." Beltoise with his shattered left elbow, insisted that

the surgeons set it in exactly the right position so that he could hold the wheel properly.

Beltoise had been halted in his tracks and hadn't proved anything yet. Logically his career had stopped there, round that bend at Rheims. All the more so since René Bonnet, now ruined and exhausted, had just sold the garage to a new company, Matra. Everything was slipping through Beltoise's fingers. Matra, an armaments company, considered racing as a means of promoting the company. Eric Offenstadt, in charge of setting up the new stable, was also a defector from motorbikes and thought that Beltoise was very good. He encouraged the boss, Jean-Luc Lagardère, to meet him. It was a job interview in a hospital! What Lagardère saw was a seriously injured person who would be left with terrible after-effects from his accident. But beyond that he saw a fighter with a will of iron; he saw a winner and hired him. In 1965, Beltoise and Matra were French champions in F3; there then

1968 was Beltoise's first complete F1 season; he finished runner-up to Zanvoort in the rain. He was among those rare drivers who could take advantage of rain.

A rare picture, taken in the Sixties: Beltoise relaxed. France's best-known driver poses with Guy Marchand and Frank Alamo, who were famous for other reasons, and who did not risk their lives every weekend.

followed F2, the very high-level endurance races with the extraordinary V-12, and finally seven full F1 seasons, with some of the best moments any driver can ever dream of, for example a sublime victory in the rain at Monaco. Everything had been proved. His original claim had indeed been legitimate.

A true driver's commitment affects all areas of life, even his friendships, with men who are always rivals; on the tracks, in the stands, and in the rarer intervals of life, the driver pushes his pawns around to get a better machine, to drive in better competitions, to ensure he has a good position in the stable. All those he talks to are of the same ilk, and of course they are all rivals, even—and above all—his teammates. All that brings them together also separates them. The driver is a wolf for other drivers.

In 1966, when Beltoise had just made his breakthrough, François Cevert arrived on the scene. He was big, handsome, educated, a pianist and the son of a jeweler. He also drove fast, and was therefore a rival. Cevert's sister Jacqueline, who had the same sunny physique, was at once attracted to Beltoise, and they married in 1968. Together within the Matra endurance team, Cevert and Beltoise, the two brothers-in-law, never stopped vying with each other, car against car, even when Matra put them in the same team, trying constantly to get a better lap record than the other.

They fought each other in Formula 1, too, one with Tyrrell, the other with BRM, until François was killed, one Saturday in October 1973, in the last Grand Prix trials. The next day Beltoise was present for the start. From the moral point of view he was reproached for being hard-hearted, but from the sporting point of view it was recognized that he was mentally strong, one of the most important conditions of the job.

A driver brushes with death and, above all else, he has to race again, or else he isn't a driver.

Jean Rédélé
1922-2007

First on the Rope

Starting from the base camp that was his father's Renault car agency, Rédélé scaled the heights of his chosen career. With Automobiles Alpine, the business he named after his beloved mountains, he opened the way for the Renault company's sporting career.

Jean Rédélé was born in Dieppe, a long way from the mountains. His family was not a local one: his father was one of those entertainers that automobile racing had spawned. Originally from Tourcoing, his keenness got him enrolled into the new Renault team, where he was Ferenc Szisz's mechanic, a new role in the first French Grand Prix, which were run in Dieppe in 1907 and 1908. It was there that Rédélé senior returned after the Great War to set up a taxi service, then a Renault agency. The genes were powerful, but World War II destroyed much: his father's agency was razed to the ground during Allied air raids.

Jean earned his daily bread by selling secondhand cars and acting as secretary to a member of Parliament, thus financing his engineering studies. For his end-of-studies internship he went to Renault. He was required to write a report, so he wrote a pamphlet about the way the newly state-owned Renault was functioning, a bold act which forced the hand of fate: his frankness and his liveliness were appreciated. Given the links the family had with the company, he was given the opportunity to re-establish the agency at Dieppe. The young man asked to be allowed to think about it for twenty-four hours. He had a stormy night discussing the matter with his father: yes, the young man would settle down into his family's line of business but he would only be

renting the space. He thus combined his personal independence with the satisfaction of continuing the family tradition, which were two essential points for him. That was not the end of it: there would have to be Renaults for sale! Only a few thousand of the Juvaquatre came out of Billancourt in 1946. In 1947, the 4CV arrived, but only a few at a time. In the middle of his agency, which was open to the elements, Jean did up GMCs, Dodges, and Jeeps, and chased orders from one corner of France to the other, and beyond: he equipped the Port at Abidjan and the Prefecture in Guyana with them. In the race to sell to the state, he wore out his 4CV doing 60,000 miles (100,000 km) in a year without any highways, with few lights, and with a 65 mph (105 km/h) top speed. This was enough to convince anyone that progress had to be made in the car industry; it was also enough for him to perfect his driving, particularly going downhill.

This was in 1950. Shortages had now reached the point of ideal equilibrium (business-wise), i.e. production had restarted, but everything that was produced was being fought over. His small business was now profitable, so Rédélé allowed himself the luxury of taking part in competitions: Le Mans, the Mille Miglia, Monte Carlo: just so many (category) wins with his 4CV. This was old-style rallying: marathons alternating with faster moments, economic acrobatics based on starting

A 4CV Renault and a suit and tie: all you needed for racing at the beginning of the fifties. The sign in the background says: The Corsair; and perhaps Jean Rédélé had a touch of the pirate about him.

and classification fees. He claimed to have been doped; in mid-race, his German rivals, former Luftwaffe pilots, had slipped him a mysterious miraculous "anti-falling-to-sleep" product!

Other magic ideas tore the 4CV from its menial condition. With a Claude five-speed instead of the original three-speed gearbox, the new engine settings very quickly boosted the poor, original 17 bhp. Over the years, Rédélé acquired the skills needed for being a driver, a company manager and a technician; and now Alpine was ready to start. In 1955, after a few "Specials," the A106 (a reference to Renault's codes for the 4CV: 1061, 62, 63, etc.) was brought out. The car was very simple, but everything had had to be invented; even the fiber glass had been bought in America!

Fifty or so Alpines came out every year, molded at Saint-Maur at CG's, and put together in the Rue Forest in Paris. In 1960, Rédélé regrouped the different operations at Dieppe. Like Chapman with Lotus, Lyons with Jaguar or Ferry Porsche, Rédélé was a boss who took an active part in all aspects of the business. On the technical side, he had the right feeling for the beam chassis; on the construction side, he was careful with the sturdiness of his cars, which were definitely very light, but reinforced in all the right places; they stood up to all the roads and aged very well; for style he guided Michelotti's pencil. On the other hand he didn't drive any more, and his Alpines climbed the ladder to success without him in the single-seater class (F3, F2, and some F1 projects), in endurance (especially Le Mans), and above all in rallies. What followed was glorious success and therefore is well known, but also less personal. His cars won the first World Championship in 1973, but that coincided with Alpine's takeover by Renault.

Jean Rédélé's office in the Rue Forest in Paris is still there, surrounded by the agency that saw the production of the first Alpines. Somebody, somewhere deep within Renault marketing, decided one day to wind Alpine up, but the Dieppe factory is still there, and that was to be Rédélé's last pride and joy.

Taking off and the summit. The Alpines, at first simple Renaults
done up and re-bodied, very quickly became formidable racing machines.
They won the first rally world championship in 1973.

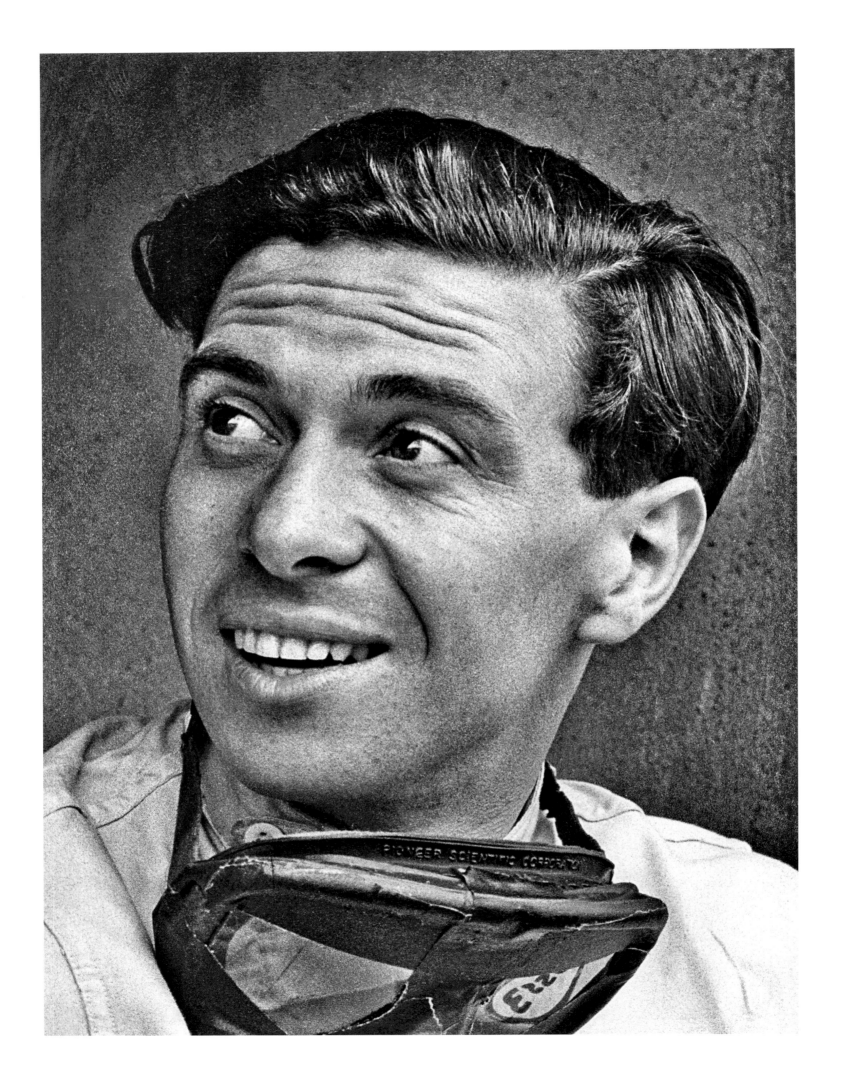

Jim Clark
1936-1968

Gentleman Jim

Whenever people draw up lists to decide the best racing driver of all time, Jim Clark is always well placed, if not top. But these aren't lists of skills, but a collection of people whose common denominator was their enthusiasm for cars. Jim Clark deserves a prominent place there, too, for his strange blend of self-confidence, which a winner undeniably needs, and true modesty.

Before becoming a world-famous driver and twice F1 World Champion, Jim Clark had not been obsessed by cars. In fact, he was not at all carried along by the conviction—quite abhorrent, but vital for racing drivers—that he was the best.

Jim Clark was born in the Scottish countryside at Kilmany. Imagine the family domain, a farm with 100 acres of water-soaked land, where three species of sheep and five hundred head of cattle grazed peacefully. When he was little, Jim Clark looked after the animals. He was a shepherd. How could a job be more at odds with the F1 paddocks and Monaco sunlight? Sometimes his father paid him, too: six pence an hour to drive the tractor. Cars were getting nearer. It was already a question of mastering a machine and being appreciated for how well you could drive it. At nine, he could drive the family's Austin Seven estate. Soon, from doing bunks to the nearest tracks, to bad reading (*Autosport!*), the fervor set in. What was remarkable at this stage was that Clark still dreamed of other people's exploits. Although he obviously passed his driving test as

soon as he could (aged seventeen), he merely co-piloted for Ian Scott Watson in "society" rallies, in which speed was less important than finding your way. When Watson, deeply impressed by the skill Clark showed during the short passages in which he let him take over the wheel, decided to put him in for a race at Aberdeen, Clark recalled the emotion and the butterflies he felt on the starting grid. But his mentor's instinct was justified, and the young man very quickly turned out to be faster than he was.

This was Great Britain in the Sixties: car racing wasn't as untouchable and protected as it is nowadays. The next part of the story would never have happened but for the Border Reivers, which was a car racing stable, but in the form of a club. All the members paid towards buying a car and it was only then that the group/club decided who would drive it. Instead of being over the moon when the club's bosses chose to entrust him with a powerful D Type Jaguar, Jim tried to change their minds! First of all because he thought the car was way beyond his ability, and also because he had a guilty conscience about not doing his chores on

Jim Clark, World Champion in 1963 and 1965 (facing page). At the time, like today, driving an F1 car was the most difficult thing a man could do. But it was hardly a high-tech affair: just look at the sticking tape on his goggles!

the farm. This concern never left him, and even later when he was a recognized champion, he still devoted most of his money to buying sheep to develop the family farm.

Scott Dawson put the D Type in for a race at Spa. For a first trip to the continent, racing at Spa, as connoisseurs will appreciate, is never easy. Starting there in a D Type in a race beset by showers was a terrible baptism of fire. Clark, who did not hide his nerves before the race, did not try to hide his weaknesses after it. In his memoirs[1] he very clearly admitted that he was scared stiff from the beginning to the end of the race, driving at 175 mph (280 km/h) when he'd never gone beyond 100 (160 km/h). Racing against the best—especially Paul Frère and Lucien Bianchi, who were almost born at Spa—was a moving experience for him. Without undue modesty, Clark also tells how, after a few laps, at the moment when he had got into his stride, he was overtaken by Masten Gregory's and Archie Scott-Brown's Lister-Jaguars who were fighting it out at the front of the race, skidding all over the place and so much faster than him that he heard them catching up with him and felt his car shake in their slipstream. "I was completely discouraged. I'd never imagined you could drive so fast." A few days later the danger from the rain over Spa (the circuit is so long that it can be raining on a bend but be dry on the straight section before) completely threw Archie Scott-Brown, who died of his injuries the following day. Clark only finished eighth, but for him this race counted as one of his initiation steps. On the other hand, he still had to trade the wheel of Jaguar for that of his combine harvester!

Although he never actually decided to make racing his main job, and was continually being told off by his family for being absent from the farm, Jim Clark managed to reach Formula 1. Those times were quite different. Engagements were almost on a piecemeal, freelance basis, for one race after another. When Clark finished third in the 1960 Le Mans 24 Hours race, right in the middle of six Ferraris, it was still with the Border Reivers, and the staff in the stands were still Scottish farmers.

The world was on the threshold of making huge leaps forward technically, though, carrying the entire car sports profession—and Formula 1

in particular—with it. Clark was in the forefront of this change with Colin Chapman and his Lotuses. As bold as he was inventive, Chapman was the first to follow in Cooper's footsteps and fit the engines in the rear. He upset the technical side of the sport even more with the Lotus 25 (or XXV), a tiny, extremely light monocoque that ran rings around the dinosaurs during the 1962 season. Behind the wheel sat, or rather lay, Jim Clark. The idea was to reduce the car's volume so that it weighed less and so that its aerodynamics were better. Chapman even had design ideas, daring to modify the cockpit. A few years earlier, Moss, Fangio, and Trintignant could still be seen holding their heavy Mercedes, Maseratis, and Ferraris in long slides, letting go of the huge steering wheels and letting them spin back by themselves before grasping them at precisely the right moment to block the wheels in exactly the right direction, to the millimeter. In the Lotus 25, Clark could be seen holding the wheel tightly from one end of the lap to the other,

The childlike joy of feeling you're the best driver in the world, and the best constructor: here Chapman shares the laurel wreaths with Clark.

crossing his arms over round the bends so as not to let go, the right hand escaping as briefly as possible to change gears, with lightning double-declutching. Technology changed driving forever. The Lotus 25 made racing enter as yet untried ground, a new kind of Formula 1, which then had to be thought out again from scratch.

The Lotus 25 appeared in May 1962 at the Monaco Grand Prix, and there was no lack of sarcastic comments. Before it can prove that it is better than established solutions, a technical innovation is always regarded with suspicion, or—if it is as radical as the monocoque was—with irritation, even. If you start to imagine that your rival's discovery might indeed work, you may as well throw out all the work you've done. Apart from the structure itself, it was Jim Clark's position, lying down "like a holidaymaker on the beach," between three fuel tanks, which either upset or surprised people. Once he got used to the pointers from this new position, he wondered how he had ever been able to drive a racing car in any other way.

The ultimate tribute was that most of the 1963 cars were inspired by Chapman's 25. The single-seaters were never the same again. Jim Clark never left Lotus and, in spite of several breakdowns and breakages, perhaps inherent to the Lotuses' ultra-light construction, Chapman still

maintained that any part that did not fall to pieces before the finishing line was still too heavy.

With Lotus, Clark won twenty-five Grand Prix, a record held for a long time; he also won two world titles and the Indianapolis 500. He was killed driving a Lotus in a minor race at Hockenheim.

He left the memory of a young man who was passionate and steady, as fast as the devil and always so truly modest. Why race cars if it's not for vanity? This was his answer: "At twenty-three I had not undergone anything like the racing that, say, Stirling Moss had at the same age. The sheer fun of racing, however, had taken a hold of me, plus a certain curiosity, which I still retain."[2] Gentleman Jim.

Aerodynamic support? Not yet. Extra-wide tires? Not yet! Just a very thin, light shell, and a huge engine. Clark and an official Lotus 49 on the British Grand Prix circuit in 1967.

1. *Jim Clark at the Wheel*, Arthur Barker, 1964
2. Ibid.

Colin Chapman
1928-1982

The Lotus Mysteries

When you excel in one thing, you don't have to excel in anything else. Colin Chapman was so closely identified with the building of Lotus cars that people forget that the chap drove pretty fast too!

Colin Chapman built his first car for his own use. The Lotus Mk 1 was an Austin Seven, stripped down as much as possible and lightened so that it could take part in the little competitions in the undergrowth: trials—the cheapest competitions possible. The Mk 2 was just a narrow chassis with only enough room for a little engine and two cramped seats, enclosed in bare aluminum bodywork. Mk 1 then Mk 2: this was an indication of the logical order in a story that had only just started, but why Lotus? That we will never know. Maybe Chapman already held the key to his minimalist philosophy: lightness, supple suspension, and smaller size.

At the end of the war, Colin was a young married man (he met Hazel at sixteen and for life), a recently qualified engineer, and a young pilot in the RAF, doing his military service. He retained a taste for planes, but not for discipline. To escape his humble background (his parents ran a small hotel), he sold secondhand cars, but his plan was to race, and to build his own car. His first machines were both a mount for the driver and a prototype, of which he could deliver a copy to whoever wanted one. If the car was good, he'd win, and if he was a good driver he'd demonstrate its qualities. This was a duality he would not escape for quite a while, toying for a long time with the hope of driving his own cars in races, at the highest level.

His success as a manufacturer brought him customers and among them some of the best drivers of the period. Chapman raced with his Lotuses against some of his customers, whose names enable us today to situate his driving standard: Graham Hill, Innes Ireland, and even Stirling Moss, and they weren't necessarily always in the lead, though Chapman could not hope to compare favorably for long with drivers who were devoted full time to their own racing career.

As time went by, the more Lotus grew in scope, and the less it was a question of him racing at a high level. Then, when he was called in by Tony Vandervell in 1957 as technical consultant for the new Vanwall, he thought that he might at last have an opportunity to tackle the Formula 1 races, in which Lotus hadn't yet taken part. He was put in for the trials for the French Grand Prix, on the very fast Rheims circuit, in the summer of 1956. But an accident in the trials damaged the beautiful green bodywork and, without a spare car, Chapman had to abandon the attempt. He never again had another opportunity.

The name Lotus took shape, and Chapman was at the head of an admittedly small empire but nonetheless just as structured as it was ambitious: Lotus Cars Ltd, Team Lotus Ltd, Lotus Components Ltd, Lotus Sales Ltd, Lotus Service Ltd (after-sales), Lotus Engineering Ltd (kits—his first activity), a whole galaxy for this meteor.

Colin Chapman waiting for his driver (facing page). If he won, the cap would fly up into the air to be caught by the fans. Some seasons Chapman had a huge budget for hats!

Chapman was an
inventor: monocoque,
ground effect, turbine,
ailerons. Here,
he is presenting his
double-chassis 88—
infinitely superior
and immediately banned
for its superiority.

The driver's romantic life disappeared into the distance. What was left was the businessman, stable boss, and also engineer: something to fill at least three separate, less agitated but no doubt less productive existences. Age surely dampened his keenness for driving, but Chapman now knew Jim Clark, certainly the best driver of his time. He no doubt knew in his heart of hearts that while he might have been able to equal a Graham Hill, he could have never outdone the flamboyant Scotsman. Production series cars were his main preoccupation. The Elite (a marvel, the only polyester monocoque in history) was followed by the Elan, whose name also began with an E, like every other Lotus car. Here we come face to face with a mystery. Was there an Eleanor, an Elizabeth, an Edgar hiding somewhere? With Chapman naturally being careful not to dispel the mystery, here's our theory. All the racing Lotuses simply had an order number: Mk 1, Mk 2, etc. The Elite, the first real road car (even if the preceding cars did make their own way to the race circuits by road in those carefree days), was also the first to be given a name, which was good for flattering the clientele. This was in 1957, and it was then that the Mk 11 was distinguishing itself in the races: "11," or written otherwise, Eleven. It might have seemed wise to him to bring together racetrack and road as closely as possible. It was there, from Eleven to Elite, that the bridge between the two nomenclatures was thrown, the two series of designations which have since lasted.

Traditions and armories: Chapman, a mere commoner, paid close attention to them. On the make's blazon, for lack of anything better, he interlaced his initials (ACBC for Anthony Colin Bruce Chapman) and then, as soon as the first sporting laurels of some import were gleaned, he struck the bodies of each of his cars with the insignia of victory. A laurel wreath for each championship won, like so many kills on the competition battlefield. Given the Lotuses' F1 performances, this very soon turned into a frieze along the sides of the Europes and Europas.

Colin Chapman was one of those men who are convinced that everything is far from having been invented and that progress is waiting just for them. As a result he opened up routes, as they say in mountaineering, but he also sometimes came unstuck on some of the sheer rock faces, and his career seesawed between reaching

summits and spectacular landslides both technically and financially. As far as success in F1 was concerned, there was the first monocoque (Lotus 25, 1962), the load-bearing engine (Lotus 49, 1967), ailerons (Lotus 49, 1968), the first aerodynamic F1s (Lotus 72, 1970), with ground effect (Lotus 78, 1977), but also the first to be sponsored by somebody outside the car-racing world (Gold Leaf cigarettes in 1968).

There were also some failures: 4 x 4 F1 (Lotuses 63 and 64, 1969), the turbine at Indianapolis (Lotus 56, 1968 and immediately banned), the twin-chassis car (Lotus 88, 1981, also banned). Clearly Chapman pushed his fascination with technical innovation and his disdain for tact too far sometimes.

There was a last mystery to finish with. Cars, which are an industrial adventure and therefore a political one too, attract individual passions, megalomania and the lure of gain. In the seventies, John Z. DeLorean, the former president of Pontiac, decided to found a make of his own with his own name. This project was to build luxury cars, and to get started the state had to help him. The British Treasury released £54 million to set up an ultra-modern factory in Belfast. After delays and defaults (no, the DeLorean DMC 12 will not have a V-12 but a Renault V-6; yes, it will cost more than planned; yes, it will be delivered years late), the Inland Revenue started getting interested in what was happening to the country's money. Colin Chapman, the technical consultant for the operation, was put under pressure by the investigators. It was his sudden death from a heart attack during the night of December 15, 1982 that ended the lawsuits. This death stunned the racing world, suddenly mourning the loss of surprises to come; who knew what that devil Chapman might have had in store for us?

On the other hand, lovers of mysteries will be happy. There were muffled rumors of a covered up "escape." Who knows if Chapman did not flee under a false name towards a new life? Alas, the whole idea is very unlikely. Wherever he might have set himself up, there would have been an immediate bubbling up of new inventions that would have attracted the world's attention once more. Unless, like Professor Brown and Marty McFly in the film *Back to the Future*, he'd been taken in a done-up DeLorean towards a future where technology finally becomes magic.

Jackie Stewart
(b. 1939)

Master Metronome

Crazy about driving? Jackie Stewart? Highly skilled driver? No doubt about that. But crazy? Crazy about precision then, crazy about accuracy. It's because of him that spectators and commentators had to stop relying on their impressions.

Once Jochen Rindt's Brabham, Chris Amon's Ferrari, Pedro Rodriguez's BRM, drifting outlandishly wide, had all sped past you, his Matra appeared, holding tight on the inside without the slightest movement, held on an impeccable line, at the limit of taking the bend short; it was difficult to admit that this car was making the best time. And yet, this precision instrument, the extremely lucid brain under the white helmet stamped with the Stewart clan tartan, was merely on the way to setting up the best set of records of the period: twenty-seven victories in ninety-nine Grand Prix and three world titles in Formula 1—in 1969, 1971, and 1973.

This perfection where driving itself was concerned was copied from Jim Clark but taken even further; it remained his trademark during the whole of his career. Lovers of bravado could have taken this for a certain reserve or even aloofness, but Stewart proved right from the start he was wholeheartedly committed.

He rubbed shoulders with car racing in the wake of his brother Jimmy, an enlightened amateur eight years his senior who even took part in a Grand Prix when Jackie was only fourteen. But Jackie, who didn't do anything worthwhile at school (he was dyslexic and this was not detected), was more interested in shooting; he just missed being selected for the 1960 Rome Olympic Games.

A few months later, Jackie got his hands on a set of wheels, belonging to a Marcos, which was a creation by real craftsmen, a wholly British one. On the car door was a special pseudonym, A. N. Other, painted on to deceive the watchfulness of his parents, who'd been alarmed by Jimmy's accident. In small races first, followed by the more important bigger ones, using Ken Tyrrell's F3, Jackie immediately showed how good he was at lining up all the inside points of a circuit in as straight a line as possible, to make as short a circuit as possible. With one eye half-closed, as though always getting ready to aim (actually his face was like that, it wasn't a marksman's technique), Stewart asserted his abilities and his personality, aloof and caustic.

By twenty-six, Jackie was in Formula 1. He was really a young man of his times, with long hair, sideburns, and flared pants, and in the paddocks he gave the impression of being a dilettante. He was nonetheless a serious driver, applied, analytical, and very interested in the technology. At a time when the Grand Prix weekends, less frequent than they are today, often ended with a party for the drivers, Jackie Stewart was among those who went to bed earlier than the

Jackie Stewart in the early days: open helmet and basic racing suit (facing page). He supported the development of protective clothing, full helmet and fire-proof clothing.

others; he kept fit and looked after his ability to concentrate.

With his successes ensuring a certain authority with the circuit owners and organizers, Stewart took a good look at his sport's more striking hazards, in order to reduce the number of accidents in which he saw his colleagues disappearing one by one; one day his wife Helen listed fifty deaths among her husband's colleagues and friends. Convinced that a good number of these tragedies could have been avoided, Jackie became a very active president of the Grand Prix Drivers' Association, and made a point of demanding vital circuit improvements, which had been studiously avoided up until then. Sometimes it was enough just to fell a tree growing too near the track.

Finally, it was Jackie Stewart again who first entrusted his financial interests to specialized managers, in this case the McCormack practice, which had cut its teeth in the golf and American football businesses. This was another success: Jackie was the first driver whose income carried on increasing after he retired from racing.

But the image we retain is of his perfect trajectories, repeated lap after lap to the nearest eighth of an inch, as though carried out with natural ease.

It was not surprising that it was this aspect of his talent which most influenced the art of driving. A number of drivers claim to be from his "school"— Nikki Lauda and Alain Prost, for example, who were so much more spectacular in their results than in their driving! And Jackie's son, Paul, too, although he didn't have such a colorful career behind the wheel, concentrating as he did on creating a stable toward which his father gave generously. Paul Stewart's adventure only lasted a short while (1997–99); the stable was handed over to Ford and to Jaguar when it turned out that young Paul had another battle to fight, against cancer. Remaining in harbor does not always shelter you from storms.

Jackie Stewart is no longer involved in Formula 1, but his aura has lasted and he is still a clever and much listened-to racing observer. This serious man also has an unexpectedly impressive deadpan sense of humor, capable of breaking the ice at receptions, even ones as stilted as the FIA prize-giving banquets, which is a skill that not just any old humorist possesses.

Solid on the big occasions: during the Monza Grand Prix of 1969, Stewart just beat Rindt's Lotus. Beltoise (no. 22) was third, McLaren fourth, less than two-tenths of a second behind the winner.

The two Flying
Scotsmen: Stewart
(left) World Champion in
1969, 1971, and 1973,
and Clark (right) in 1963
and 1965. After Clark's
death in 1968, Stewart
became an untiring
promoter of racetrack
safety.

Pierre Bardinon
(b. 1931)

Resistance Fighter

The man is known for his collection of racing Ferraris, the most beautiful in the world. But well before he built up his collection, he'd been bitten by the driving bug, and hard.

He has a little mustache and a smile that you might think is haughty. Pierre Bardinon is sizing you up. If it's his fortune in red cars that you venerate, then he sees you as just another gaper, curious about big and beautiful figures—so many dollars at the last auction for such and such a Ferrari—and you're therefore uninteresting. If he suspects you of being a real lover of their formal beauty, with an inconsolable yearning for the fiery events that they went through, then you are the sort of person he put this collection together for, which he did at a time when these cars had been turned over to the amateurs by the manufacturer's stable, then been outdated by new racing statutes, and ran the risk of being simply scrapped.

Bardinon, a leather industrialist with a very average fortune, acquired some of his priceless Ferraris for less than the price of the production series cars everybody was fighting over. He tells how it all happened one day in the mountains—where he had gone, not to meditate, but to take part in a hill climb—where his sirens enslaved him. The sound of the racing V-12s, sharp, singing, speaking in their own way of the countryside, long high revs, rhythmic gear-changing punctuated by dull barking, grumbling, and gurgling, and then once again the pure, harmonious, and regulated explosions that make up an engine's music, secondary but essential. He couldn't allow all that to be silenced. And so it was that Bardinon's taste for the beautiful shapes of hand-hammered bodywork preserved the collection. It certainly

wasn't for gain, or else he'd have sold off the collection during one of the periods of "red fever," when every Ferrari found a buyer at exceptional prices. Bardinon held on to his cars, even when he was offered ten, twenty, a hundred, even two hundred times the initial price, thus preserving a gallery of masterpieces so that people like us could appreciate them today. Many people simply did not realize at the time how much they were worth. This has proved to be a collective folly, since today a Ferrari is worth the price of a van Gogh, when one of them now would alone pay for the whole collection at its purchase price, and the family farm at Aubusson to boot.

When a journalist asked Enzo Ferrari why he didn't keep one example of every model, the old man answered: "There is a man in France, a certain Bardini, who does just that and does it very well, too."

In France, yes, in the Creuse, where Pierre Bardinon comes from. If this means anything, being from the Creuse is perhaps the exact opposite of what is meant by being from Paris. He is a lover of calm, space, and a certain quality of human relations, too, in the long term. On the rare occasions he orders a new car from Maranello (250LM, or 512 BB, or I 50 and 550 Maranello), he insists that they bear the chassis number 23, the registration number of the French "department" where he was born. The beautiful domain he owns is certainly enviable, but it's a long way off the more ostentatious houses he

A curator ...
Pierre Bardinon saw the value in collecting the real racing Ferraris, when the rest of the world had turned away.

could have acquired instead of his cars. One of the wings, a former stable, shelters the Ferraris in the collection. There are some Bugattis also. "When you love Bugattis, the people you love are dead. There's no risk of them betraying you," says Bardinon, who is just as demanding where friendship is concerned as he is with mechanics. It seems that once, one of the new Ferrari chairmen did not shake hands with him after he had just crossed half of Europe to bring one of his jewels to a meeting in honor of the name.... Passionately interested, always; blind *tifoso*—fan—of the brand, never.

The way society is evolving has put him on his guard; road safety laws, for example. Ever since they've been in force, he has always got round them and still finds them stupid. He buys his cars first and foremost to drive them. He goes away and comes back every weekend, traveling between the Creuse, on the northwestern border of the Massif Central, and Paris. His route used to be Guéret-Chateauroux-Vierzon-Orléans-Etampes, especially at the wheel of his 250 LM, one of the last Ferrari client-competition cars. As it requires 100-octane gas, he had organized things very privately with a cooperative gas station midway, at Salbris.

Sometimes he had to bring back the children; for a long time he used an E Type Jaguar, the Lightweight version, i.e. lightened for racing or for more incisive, more precise driving. Jaguar

had never even imagined that you could lie three children in the long rear window shelf, with just two bucket seats up front and a bolster for the little kiddies. When the kids grew bigger he found another solution: a fake ambulance, a Citroën DS station wagon with red crosses, and a turbocharger under the bonnet, in which often he overtook crawling traffic on the saturated approaches to the capital. At its wheel they glimpsed an ambulance driver wearing a white coat, devilishly fast and smiling maliciously: Pierre Bardinon. Behind him the children were finishing off their night, at 100 mph. They were never late for school.

"I had no intention of killing myself or anybody else for that matter. I must have done at least 200,000 or 250,000 miles under those conditions without incident. Be careful of the traffic? But a good driver does nothing else!"

In the 1960s, in deepest Creuse, Pierre Bardinon built a circuit according to his own design, where visiting friends can still see the Ferraris in the collection frolicking and rumbling around.

A circuit is a strange thing; it's like a laboratory of precision movement. Patrick Bardinon, Pierre's son, holds the track record there with a Formula 1 Ferrari, which had been loaned by Maranello for the occasion. This virus is of course hereditary; an inevitable product, if not the genes, of the atmosphere.

Thirty-six Ferrari GTOs were produced between 1962 and 1964, all of them winners, and now the ultimate collector's car. At this lap of honor on the Champs-Elysées, Bardinon is in the foreground on the right in his GTO 1964.

Johnny Servoz-Gavin
1942–2006

Gone in a Flash

Racing is the ideal sport for the playboy, particularly in Formula 1 and especially in Monaco. Handsome, fair-haired, and fast, "Johnny" Servoz-Gavin was just right for the part, but he found out fairly quickly what the limits to this game were.

It was May 1968 and, throughout France, the atmosphere was particularly volatile: radical students making their point in bold displays of public disorder. At some remove from France, the reaction in Monaco was hard to gauge. At any rate, although there was heckling at the Cannes Festival, the Monaco Grand Prix went on as usual.

Jackie Stewart, one of the season's favorites with his Tyrell Team's Matra, had broken his wrist so was unable to drive. Big Ken Tyrrell had sorted through all the part-time pretenders and very intuitively gave Johnny Servoz-Gavin his chance. The 1966 French F3 Champion, with several wins in the 1967 prototype races, the young devil had a good pedigree; but although his background was sound, nothing was really expected from a driver who was just starting F1, especially at Monaco! The sinuous, narrow circuit—the difficult circuit *par excellence*—hardly even gave the drivers enough space to make a mistake. The beginner took to the track, started going round—according to his peers he was the fastest at "learning" a new circuit—and at the end of the trials he was at the front of the grid! Only Graham Hill, a three-times winner there, had made a better time. By tradition, no trials take place on Saturdays in Monaco; the town is given back to the pedestrians and the drivers go to the countless cocktail parties given in their honor. Servoz-Gavin was just as much at home there as

he was on the track: his father owned a café and he himself had retained a liking for parties from the days he had spent there. On Sunday, the man whose name was on everybody's lips, this beginner who had out-timed John Surtees, Jack Brabham, and Denny Hulme—five titles between the three of them—had the nerve to get off to a better start than all the others and outdistance them at the rate of one second per lap. For three laps Johnny was the best driver in the world. Was this feeling just a bit too exhilarating? In Monaco the crash rails are close and on his fourth passage through the tunnel, the Matra's wheel brushed the rail just enough to cause mechanical problems, and he had to pull out.

In May 1970 the weather was gray and heavy. Servoz-Gavin was now well-known in the paddocks. Since the beginning of the season, he had been with Jackie Stewart at Tyrrell's, the team holding the title. Three weeks earlier, Servoz-Gavin had finished fifth in the Spanish Grand Prix in Madrid, and now here he was, back once more in Monaco, the scene of his earlier exploits. Servoz-Gavin at Monaco: the memories had not faded and great things were expected of him.

During those two years, Johnny's career had not followed the usual path. He was the flamboyant runner-up in the Monza Grand Prix and had won a European title in Formula 2; both proved that he was talented, but the Matra

Lagardère (facing page, right) was a media man. He was not averse to his drivers being handsome and their having their own personality which would make them popular.

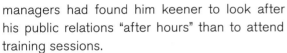
Monaco, 1970.
On the same racing
track on which he had
triumphed two years
previously, he doesn't
even succeed in
qualifying!
That evening, he gave up
competing altogether.

managers had found him keener to look after his public relations "after hours" than to attend training sessions.

It was the start of the Monaco training sessions. The scenario turned out exactly the opposite of what was expected. Servoz-Gavin didn't manage to qualify. Given the car he had (his teammate was in the pole position), it was an outrage. Tactfully, Tyrrell reminded peole that he had injured his right eye three months earlier during an off-road rally, and that this would have handicapped him on this very special circuit. But that evening, Johnny organized a cocktail party on a yacht to celebrate his non-qualification. And when the traditional Formula One-shaped cake was brought out, Johnny raised his glass and declared: "Have a good look because it's the last time you'll see me with a racing car!"

The career of Johnny Servoz-Gavin, the handsome Formula 1 driver, well and truly petered out. Gone were the restrictions and contracts, gone was the money, gone were the thrill of performance and the dread of having an accident; gone was racing—which had killed his friend Jo Schlesser, and Gerhard Mitter, Mike Spence, Ludovico Scarfiotti, and the great Jim Clark. Servoz-Gavin left Grand Prix racing of his own free will. No doubt he found other reasons to throw parties.

Brock Yates

(b. 1933)

Go West, Young Man

Was it a revolt by the well-to-do or a healthy rebellion against the diktats of an administration gone awry? Some driving enthusiasts have never gone along with the idea of speed limits. Brock Yates was a militant journalist and organized a wildcat rally on the open roads across the USA.

Brock Yates used to be a newspaperman who test-drove for a specialist magazine, *Car and Driver*. He would try out new cars as and when they came out and put them through their paces. It was actually the same type of job as a film critic, except that when a critic leaves the film theater, the film is normally still in one piece. In the case of Brock Yates, his skepticism, both professional and natural, applied to anything concerning cars—even the rules and regulations. And therefore speed limits, too.

It is common knowledge that in terms of the automobile, America was ahead of the Old Continent; the petrol engine appeared much earlier there and it was decided to curb it there earlier too. And it wasn't with half-measures either; even on the big highways, many of which are dead straight, drivers were limited to 55 mph (88 km/h), thanks to the National Maximum Speed Law. It was in fact a Federal Law, whose aim was to cut gas consumption following the 1973 oil crisis: the target was 2 percent; the officially evaluated result less than 1 percent.

Naturally this progress was also made in the name of road safety. Just as obvious, and acknowledged as such by the police departments who analyze the causes of accidents, was the fact that the foremost reason for road accidents

had become drowsiness and fatigue caused by the staggering lengths of journeys, in a country spanning more than 2,800 miles (4,500 km) from east to west and more than 1,500 miles (2,500 km) from north to south.

Brock Yates thought these measures were totally inept and decided to prove how absurd they really were. In fact, he decided to organize a secret wildcat rally between New York and Redondo Beach, California; the idea was to drive as fast as possible, but driving "at the most suitable speed." And this was the problem in a nutshell: speed limits impose a standard, arbitrary speed on all drivers, whatever the car, whatever the weather, whatever mood the driver is in. Yates wanted to let each driver decide for himself what the speed limits ought to be, based on his own circumstances, instead of simply believing himself safe as soon as he started obeying the law, which is surely the most dangerous of beliefs.

He christened his trial "Cannonball," as a tribute to Erwin Baker, whose nickname it was and who, between 1910 and 1930, had set coast-to-coast records on all sorts of mounts, for the builders. Yates was happy to emphasize that America's traffic, the symbol of conquest and freedom of movement, was going to slow down

Irresponsible joker or useful humanitarian? Brock Yates (facing page) invented the Cannonball to show the debilitating character and the long-term danger of speed restrictions.

Cannonball was originally
the nickname for Erwin
Baker, a brave marathon
driver who made driving
across the United States
on behalf of the car
makers before
World War II a specialty.

for the first time, and that even the paltry cars of the Twenties had been able to reach average speeds way above 55 mph (88 km/h).

The Cannonball rules were very simple: "Each competitor puts himself down for the race with his own choice of car and reaches the finishing line by his own route. The one with the shortest time wins." No fixed itinerary, just a (secret) departure point in New York City and an arrival point at Redondo Beach, California.

Let's go straightaway to the upshot of the story: all went well. There were no accidents during the three Cannonballs organized in 1972, 1975, and 1979. The winners, all unofficial of course, were awarded a trophy. It had only sentimental value and was made of tools welded together, a sort of primitive and deliberately laughable Oscar. The best time, coast to coast, was 32 hours and 51 minutes: an average of 84 mph (134.4 km/h). Overall, this thumb-your-nose-at-the-law event, this road-safety-correct-thinking happening, produced a considerable effect. It inspired four films—Brock Yates appeared in one, playing not himself but a policeman spouting all that policemen do spout when shown how inept some laws are and how futile their own jobs are enforcing them. But these films, these pleasant, stunt-filled, B-film slapstick movies, did the cause more harm than good. They didn't show the real negative effects of speed limits: speeding is the only thing the police want to check (it's easy and profitable); it obsesses the police and warps the judgment of drivers who, though pestered by propaganda do care about obeying, but forget to make sure they are actually safe when driving carefully and flexibly. Not to mention the dizzy

increases in travel time, drowsiness, and fatigue. It's a disaster. Despite Brock Yates's iconoclastic efforts, every year there are more than forty thousand deaths on the road in the States, proportionally more even than in France where speed limits are much less draconian, and more than Germany too, where there is no speed limit at all on some motorways.

In one of the films inspired by his adventure, Brock Yates (left) plays the part of a policeman. Here he is pictured with the director Hal Needham and the actor Dom de Luise.

Gilles Villeneuve
1950-1982

The Will o' the Wisp

He had the fieriest temperament in the history
of modern F1; the most flamboyant, finely honed talent.
His destiny was reaching melting point.

He was the fastest driver in the world but not the driver with the most titles: only six victories in the F1 World Championship. As a driver he wasn't the best strategist either: "overtaking somebody in the pits" thanks to a more clevery planned refueling moment, wasn't up his street at all. Nor was he the best technician: nobody has ever maintained that Villeneuve had good technical ideas that allowed car design to progress. Sorry, yes he did: the Ferrari engineers said that thanks to him they learned how to make solid gearboxes! Neither was he the most ingratiating of drivers: drawing up a budget, courting the stable bosses and unearthing the best car were not part of his range of talents. He wasn't the most diplomatic of drivers, either; he didn't know how to explain away poor performances or express just the slightest suspicion about his opponents' results. No, these were not among Gilles Villeneuve's skills. He was simply the fastest driver of his age.

Once aboard a car, no matter which one, Gilles Villeneuve at once felt what speed he could get out of it. Never was Gilles outdone by another competitor driving the same type of car round one lap.

And the spectators adored him—all the public, the chauvinists from all over the world, the fans of this driver and of that multiple champion; no spectator who ever saw one of Gilles's grand circuits could do anything else but like the guy. Gilles gave his all for racing, all for speed. He was a magnificent acrobat, somebody who opened doors, who pushed back the limits of human talent for everybody.

His skills had been developed on the snow bikes and skidoos of his youth in Quebec (a discipline in which he was 1974 World Champion), and as it turned out was transferable to all machines—not only cars, but also the planes and helicopters that he piloted without trying, performing the most picturesque and spectacular maneuvers. There are such a lot of memorable moments that it's well nigh impossible to choose the best examples.

There was that Atlantic Formula Grand Prix where he got the better of all the Formula 1 drivers who had been invited to the race, among them James Hunt, on his way to winning the world title. It was James Hunt, a good sport, who in fact opened F1's doors for him.

There was also that Grand Prix in which Gilles burst one of his Ferrari's rear tires. He made a point of bringing the car back to the pits, and ended the lap almost as quickly as if he had had four tires. Obviously, when he drew up in front of them, the mechanics could pack away their new tire, couldn't they? The rear axle unit had almost been torn off. The cars were never tough enough for Gilles.

There was the 1981 Spanish Grand Prix when his Ferrari was the fastest car on the grid in a straight line but the slowest round the bends. Gilles nevertheless succeeded in holding the

With an almost slender silhouette, but with inexhaustible energy, Gilles Villeneuve (facing page) was only able to drive giving his all.

whole of the grid at bay and got the closest win in history, with five cars ending the race at his heels without ever being able to overtake him.

There was the 1979 Dijon Grand Prix in which René Arnoux in his Renault Turbo caught up with him; Gilles held him off for three laps until Arnoux suffered fuel problems and was forced to let him go. Off the track, over the limit, on the vibrators, on the grass, with jammed wheels, rubbing wheels—it was the most beautiful duel that the F1 cameras had ever filmed. The Ferrari and the Renault, carried away at abnormal speeds, danced together in a reckless but fair fight. And once the checkered flag was lowered, the two men, still level with each other and slowing down at last, in the end simply saluted each other with a wave of the hand. This shot made up for many boring hours in front of the TV set watching insipid, cautious, and uninspiring Grand Prix races.

There were also those qualifying rounds for the US Grand Prix, on the Watkins Glen circuit in pouring rain, during which he got the best times; better than his teammate in an equivalent car, by eleven seconds!

With such driving, how do you account for Villeneuve winning so little in F1? On one hand it was proof that all the other skills, the ones Gilles didn't have, do play an important role in building a World Champion. Another part of the answer, a big part, is to be found in the word "fairness." For Gilles, having a contract as second driver was no problem. He was successively Carlos Reutemann's and Jody Scheckter's second and helped them reach their objectives. It was also what would go some way to explaining his anger after the 1982 Imola Grand Prix, during which his teammate but also his friend, Didier Pironi, overtook him after the stable bosses had told them to "hold their positions."

From then on, it was open warfare. The little Quebecois swore in front of witnesses to shut the great Didier Pironi's trap for him.

He never spoke to him again. As they were both members of the Scuderia, and their Ferraris easily dominated everybody else that year, there wasn't any doubt as to who would win the title. During the next Grand Prix, in Belgium, the struggle began with the trial sessions. Gilles wanted the pole position. In the middle of his fast lap, he bumped into Jochen Mass's March when he was slowing down. Jochen misunderstood and, to let him pass, pulled over to the side on which Gilles had chosen to overtake. The Ferrari took off and broke up. Some drivers said that Gilles's last thought would most likely have been to regret this botched lap.

Enzo Ferrari liked committed pilots, pilots who would fight their way to the top. He adored Gilles, who spent his entire Formula 1 career at Ferrari.

Monaco, 1981,
Gilles ready to attack,
as always.
Gilles inspired more
than admiration,
something closer
to adoration from
the general public.
There is even today
a cult around
his number 27.

Steve McQueen

1930-1980

The King of Cool

Do you normally associate Steve McQueen with a sawn-off Winchester? If so, that's cinema. His passion was first and foremost driving. Through his acting, and the films that he influenced as both star and even producer, he was just the sort of mentor that the sport needed.

In the United States, Steve McQueen's immoderate love of speed and driving was so proverbial that in the comic strip, *Cars*, the main character was called McQueen. A keen interest in cars can start early, but it takes shape when you are of an age to start driving. Born in 1930, abandoned by his father, a member of a flying circus, then by his mother, who gave him to some farmers, Terence Steve McQueen had a difficult and turbulent youth, with several stays in a reformatory. He broke the vicious circle by joining the army at seventeen. When he left the Marines in 1952 it was to study at The Actors' Studio and to blow his first fees by buying cars and motorbikes. It was during that dazzling period when European sports cars (Triumph, MG, Porsche, etc.) appeared on American soil and the Americans responded to this straightforward aggression. Not to mention the motorbikes: Triumph again, Norton, Vincent, followed by the Japanese soon afterwards.

Having become famous under the name of Josh Randall in *Dead or Alive*, McQueen bought all sorts of machines. And the crafty fellow also had the producers buy, for various reasons, the machines that he wanted. He took part in local races in California with a Porsche 356 Speedster, then with a Lotus XI, which was a difficult car

and good for refining his driving technique; and he won some of them. When he was in Europe shooting a film he tried out the Mini Cooper S in his spare time. He did a somersault with it, but was suitably adroit and tactful for John Cooper to imagine what he could get out of this American star: he offered him a factory car straight off! During the 1962 Sebring 3 Hours race for production series cars, in which his teammates for the race were some of the great names—Innes Ireland, Stirling Moss, and Pedro Rodriguez—he drove a small Healey Sprite. He finished ninth at the wheel of this humble car. He had a go at the single-seaters in a junior formula, but without great success.

He collected machines, or rather he accumulated them. Was he bulimic or epicurean? Both. As a dabbler in everything, he bought all sorts of cars, hundreds of bikes, but also planes and even loads of pickups. It was a collection of sorts, but rather made up of the multifarious, exciting, and often surprising milestones in the life of a sensualist. After going round so many bends, these machines all made their last journey together, to satisfy a fervent interest that was always swirling around searching, always varied, always leaping from one style to another, with a passion for one particular Jaguar XK SS,

Perhaps weary of always acting at being the best, McQueen (facing page) took part in and won real races, without tricks or understudies.

one of sixteen examples produced a short while before the Jaguar factory was totally burnt down. McQueen kept it for ten years, then gave it to the Reno Museum, then bought it back ten years later, obviously for a much higher price!

In any case, on the screen, just as John Wayne had his horses, Steve had his cars, some of which became just as much of a legend as he did.

An actor can do much more than just act in the films he's in. It's clear that Steve McQueen's never-ending fixation with cars in daily life had an influence on a number of his roles.

So it was in *The Thomas Crown Affair*. In the title role he was a strict, wealthy, and slightly secretive businessman, maybe just a little bit of a burglar. This psychological thriller had a woman insurance investigator getting under the tycoon's feet. She was another strong character, played by Faye Dunaway. The film is obviously a courtship display in which the two protagonists spar with each other charmingly and intelligently. Among Crown/McQueen's talents was his skill at driving all sorts of machines. We learn from him that you can take a lot of risks in a glider. In town, the businessman drives a Rolls-Royce, the suitable accessory for the film. The other car that made a strong impression was the buggy, which went through a series of uninhibited, artistic leaps among the dunes. It was actually the counterpoint to the screeching Rolls-Royce, an obvious clue to Crown's dual personality. It was McQueen who had the buggy built, giving it the complex and lofty task of expressing freedom of spirit and also good fortune. As a base he chose a Meyers Manx, the august ancestor of all buggies, invented by Bruce Myers himself. If the chassis was the classic stripped-down Beetle, the engine was no longer the nice flat four, but a Corvair flat six. It was the perfect example of McQueen's involvement in a film. As he had to play a character, the actor gave him

his own interests and decided how Crown would have chosen a suitable car, then driven it "with his hands," i.e., quite differently from what the script had indicated originally. Since McQueen had a switch on board which operated the camera and chose its direction, it could be said he was an actor-stuntman-producer. A word for Faye Dunaway, who wasn't at all frightened of shooting most of the action scenes herself in the wild buggy. She was indeed supposed to be more than an amateur, since she drove a straw-colored 275 GTS, which was enough to situate the role she was playing and dishearten the viewers who had fallen under Miss Dunaway/Anderson's spell. McQueen liked the buggy so much that he bought it when the film was finished.

Bullitt was made the same year. Remember that McQueen was involved both as actor and as the boss of his own company, Solar Productions. Where the script consisted of one line—the famous car-chase scene—Steve's interpretation marked his own legend, and action cinema's and also Ford's. Ford wasn't that keen at first because all the Ford and Mustang logos had been taken off the car. Today, Ford continues to exploit Jack Bullitt's spirit, going so far as to bring Steve McQueen back to life to sell the Puma, and putting the film's name on naturally rather special Mustangs.

To the question, "How do you make it look like the cars are going fast?" somebody gave the

The film and real life: at the wheel of this Corvair-engined Buggy, Steve McQueen played the role of Thomas Crown, and this consisted of driving very fast, with Faye Dunaway beside him.

hitherto rather unsuspected answer: "By filming them going really fast!" Where a conventional cameraman would have used side shots or maybe undercranked the camera, someone else suggested that a long sequence without the slightest camera movement was both more realistic and more spectacular. That someone was Steve McQueen, and he did not stop at just suggesting.

Bullitt was certainly the first film in which a car's suspension was shot in action going round a bend and in cinemascope. The suspension was of course prepared at McQueen's request as usual. Naturally you don't get over a vice just like that, and the long chase does have its more naïve moments, like the jumps down the San Francisco streets. But overall, this sequence set a new, long-lasting standard of quality in cinema. The stuntmen now just had to get on with the job.

It was at Sebring again in 1970 that a Porsche 908, entered by Solar Productions for Steve McQueen and Peter Revson, just missed first place! In the end, McQueen was runner-up behind Mario Andreotti. In a less important race at Phoenix, he even won.

Racing cars and making films led naturally to the idea of making a film paying tribute to the art of driving. It was *Le Mans*, made in 1971, in which cars played the main roles. It was both a financial adventure and a technical challenge. Steve shot this film partly so as to have the pleasure of lining up for the Le Mans 24 Hours, but the film's insurers forbade him even to think of taking part. What remained was a film with rather a thin and scarcely credible storyline, but whose shots are now watched over and over again on fans' screens. McQueen certainly made films that better revealed his acting skills, like *Papillon* and *Getaway*, etc.

Sudden death always leaves a strong impression, and for a man of action it is always sad, even more so when it seems to prove that

those who are timid in life are right. Sudden death seems to bear out all those discouraging warnings like "you'll hurt yourself," or even the shameful, "I told you so, didn't I?" which has a satisfying aftertaste for all those who never dare do anything. Steve McQueen's death from a common illness at the age of fifty was, on the contrary, an encouragement to live life to the full beforehand, and even as fully as possible.

The beret is a tribute to France: the photograph was taken at Le Mans, where Steve McQueen was shooting the film of the same name.

Jean-Claude Andruet
(b. 1942)

In No Particular Order

He racked up a formidable tally, and had a long career, certainly;
but although rally-goers loved Andruet a great deal,
it was more for his capacity to clock up unearthly times,
to open up the road, to break records.

A competent factory driver must be reliable, clock up points at the end of each race, and obtain the best results possible for the car. Andruet followed this model a few times. But if he is among the best rally-men in the world today, it's above all because of his feats. Jean-Claude Andruet often went off the track, sometimes missed victories that were his for the taking. But he won others, unexpected ones, in the most unpredictable way possible. He was a real livewire of a driver, a quick-tempered man, operating on the edge of folly.

Jean Todt, who was a much sought-after and renowned rally copilot, recalled one incident, in *Echappement* magazine. "I always understood what my drivers were doing. When we were going round a bend and suddenly I didn't understand any more, it meant we were going to go off the road in the next second. During a *Neige et Glace* rally with Andruet, we crossed a mountain pass at a speed that was quite definitely beyond my understanding. I had never seen it before, and I have never seen it since."

This was an eyewitness account that said it all; Jean Todt has since proved to what extent sagacity applied to car sports could be effective. Todt forged the personalities of his more ebullient drivers (Ari Vatanen, Michael Schumacher and so on) and knew how to channel their talents

for the greater good of his employers—Peugeot, then Ferrari. When faced with the brute force of a rough diamond like Andruet, Todt admitted he was disarmed. You could say it was reason paying a tribute to genius, or perhaps madness.

In the 1973 Monte Carlo rally, the race was going to be won by the Alpine-Renaults, but which one? They were at daggers drawn until the last special, the Col de la Madone, for which the record was 16 minutes and 3 seconds. This time Jean Todt teamed up with Ove Andersson, the Swede. They clocked up a record time, smashing the record by forty seconds: 15 minutes and 23 seconds! Had they won the race? Andersson was already delighted with his victory. Todt was waiting next to the timekeepers' table. Andruet hadn't arrived yet. The little blue Alpine suddenly burst round the last bend at a speed which was quite amazing, beating Andersson's time by twelve seconds. On the Col de la Madone, they still talk of Andruet's miracle.

What sort of person was Andruet? He was an enthusiast in everything. At fifteen, he wanted to go into holy orders, but at sixteen he was married and at eighteen a family man; you can add to all this an insatiable appetite for work and action. When he was still young, after his hours at school, he helped out in his mother's little restaurant in Montreuil, in the inner working-class suburbs of Paris. To earn a little

Laughter and fear in
equal measures. Andruet
(facing page) turned
his many passions into
a driving force.

pocket money, he did all sorts of jobs, collected and sold old newspapers, helped in a hardware store, opened oysters, etc.

When he grew up, he was a rep (no hours, no limits, and lots of driving), and at the same time found the time to play judo, a sport in which he became the 1961 French champion in the lightweight category.

Andruet was already twenty-four when he met a customer looking for a teammate for a regional rally with his very recent Renault 8 Gordini. Andruet was bitten by the racing bug and he never lost it. His rise was marked by unexpected exploits and failures, and brutal drops of morale. Andruet is perhaps the most emotional and fragile man to be found at such a high level. The smallest incident can get him down; any mistake can cause him to have doubts. But faced with a really nasty blow or a big delay, he was capable of doing the impossible. He was even seen with a flat tire during the Tour de Corse!

But in his normal state Andruet was already a very good driver; someone to beware. His five French and European titles bear witness to this, and it wasn't by whiling away his time in ditches that he won the Monte Carlo rally, the Tour de Corse (three times), the Tour de France for cars (three times), and the Cévennes Criterium (four times); his endurance results also prove his ability to focus: it was not by being "beside yourself" during the 24 Hours that you win the Performance Index, or have a category win (three times) at Le Mans.

Yes, Le Mans! Andruet shared that rare ability with Jean Ragnotti and Vic Elford of being just as fast on the circuits as in the rallies. He was just as demanding as he was flighty; he had experienced everything and driven everything: Alpines of course, but also Lancia Stratos, Alfa Romeo 2000s, Ferrari Daytonas, Ferrari 308 GTBs, Lancia 037s, single-seaters, circuit runabouts, great GTs, etc.

But it is the most intense scenes that leave the most durable mark on people's memories. Anduret was driving the Ferrari 308, dancing round the bends and literally taking off above the winding tarmac in the Cevennes. It was a tribute to his female teammates. Indeed, Jean-Claude often had women copilots (Peuvergne, Veron, Rick, Emmanuelli, Sappey, Bouchetal, and especially "Biche" Petit).

Today Andruet, who was a gas guzzler but also a lifelong ecologist (of the truly committed kind), has founded an electric car and bike company. This does not prevent him from racing with period cars. And, if it hadn't been for a mechanical breakdown, he might even have stood a chance at winning the 2009 Tour de Corse.

Andruet at the 1972 Tour de Corse, driving with his copilot "Biche" Petit.

Andruet's career
followed the rally
arms race, from the
frail Alpines to the
formidable Lancia
037s, by way of—in
particular—this Fiat 131
Abarth.

Graham Hill

1929-1975

The Queen's Musketeer

You can recognize a driving fanatic by how young he is when he starts driving, how dazzling his career is, and how uncompromising his vocation is. But Graham Hill passed his driving test at twenty-four, started racing in earnest at twenty-seven, and throughout his life he kept up a slightly mocking attitude towards his career, as if he would have been just as happy doing something else entirely.

In fact the reason he started driving so late in life was because he was in the Royal Navy, and Her Majesty's sailors don't often have the opportunity to try their hand at racing cars. As for being a born competitor, Hill had already shown that he had ambition, but for rowing, not racing. An enthusiast for the sport all his life, he wore the colors of his club, the London Rowing Club, on his famous dark blue helmet with white stripes. And on land, it was scrambling that attracted him first.

He found out he liked driving when a friend took him to try out a single-seat trainer at five shillings a lap. Thrilled by the experience, Hill was determined to become a professional driver. He raced cars and, to get closer to the machines that attracted him like a magnet, he got a job as a mechanic with the Lotus team, founded by designer and engineer Colin Chapman. Did Chapman recognize in him a man with the mindset of the double world champion he was soon to become? Not at all, though admittedly it must be said in Chapman's defense that at the time everybody was driving the cars, including Chapman to start with. On Friday evenings most of the workers at the tiny Lotus factory would scatter, looking for a friendly circuit where they could show off their talent at the wheel of a car, very often completely unpretentious models. Racing was then an elegant pastime, and for the most talented of these mercenaries, it was just possible to earn a living from it, or at least to get a good return on the price of a machine. And Graham Hill, the late starter, was the most regular. He traded driving circuits for hours in the workshop, and if he was lucky enough to win some competition or other, driving any sort of vehicle, he put aside the few guineas to support his family; he had married Bette, a member of the rowing club like him. They had three children.

Graham Hill very quickly revealed what a versatile driver he was. He was just as much at ease driving a single-seater racing car as he was a sedan, and he was willing to accept any engagements, any adventures. The temptation of money went some way to explaining this, but his taste for driving and for combat was certainly the stronger motivation.

Long hair and sideburns—the former Navy Engine Room Artificer and rowing champion welcomed the relaxed attitude of the Sixties.

Graham had a soldier's boldness or, better, that of those swashbucklers for whom a duel was another opportunity to prove your worth, but above all he liked to have fun. He wasn't the type to pull his punches. The stranger it was, the more excited he got; for instance, he was offered the chance to try out the new turbine car at Le Mans; its inertia would have posed several problems to a lot of other drivers. "There was quite a time lag on both the positive and negative accelerations. When the turbine was ticking over, there was a three second lag before it set off again. Inversely, when the throttle was shut and the car braked sharply, it took three seconds for the turbine to start to tick over again. When we got to Mulsanne, we started to brake with the left foot, lifting the right from the gas pedal. Then a hundred yards before the hairpin, we accelerated with the right foot and just before going into the bend we lifted the left foot from the brake. It was a question of getting the power at exactly the right moment, neither too early nor too late." It was rather a risk.

Although he started his career relatively late in life, Hill enjoyed a long stint in racing.

When a puncture took him out of the 1969 US Grand Prix race, breaking both his legs, many commentators and opponents thought the time had come for him to retire. He had already raced eleven full Formula 1 seasons and carried off two world titles. But Hill returned for a further five Grand Prix seasons. And, although he didn't win any more Formula 1 races, his dedication surprised a great number of younger drivers. Henri Pescarolo admitted that when the Matra team chose "old glory" as his teammate for the 1972 Le Mans 24 Hours, his first thought was that he'd been deprived of victory in advance. But on the contrary, he realized that Hill was a motivated teammate, attentive and devilishly gifted. Twenty-four hours later he opened a bottle of champagne with the man he had almost scorned. The fact was that Graham had particularly wanted to win the 24 Hours race, since it would complete his Triple Crown. Along with the Indianapolis 500 and the Monaco Grand Prix, it was one of the best-known and most prestigious races as far as the general public was concerned. He'd already achieved victory in both the others. At Monaco, the man with the mustache had even been able to shake hands with Prince Rainier and present his respects to Princess Grace, five times in fact.

Had he managed to tame the circuit? No, he found it just as hard as anybody else; it's just that difficulty spurred him on.

When, eventually, his times began to slow down compared with the new generation in Formula 1, who were driving faster cars than his, Hill began to think of a future beyond driving. In 1973 he created a Formula 1 team under his own name and started a new career as team manager. Meanwhile he had unearthed a young, promising British talent, Tony Brise; he was getting ready to show him round with the usual good humor and trust in good luck that had characterized his own career. But on a late November night, returning from France with five colleagues, he crashed his Piper Aztec plane in thick fog on Arkley Golf Course in north London. Hill, team manager Ray Brimble, Tony Brise and three other members of the team were all killed.

Among the drivers you can recognize a driving fanatic by how early he starts driving, how dazzling his career is and how intransigent his passion is. And also by the strength of the influence he has. His young son, Damon, much to the initial despair of his mother Bette—but then with her backing, as she had recognized true vocation—also chased after the Formula 1 World Championship, which he won in 1996, before taking his bow more serenely.

Graham Hill,
Colin Chapman
and the Lotus 49
in 1967.

From the Eighties

Chasing Progress

The car is now master of the world. It has transcended everything, simplified everything, and spoilt everything. Its reign has all but taken away the pleasure of driving. It has overwhelmed towns, and it has reshaped the countryside with its motorways—those saddened realms of steady and forbidden speed. Our adventures behind the wheel are not quite what they used to be.

The magical object that is the car has, however, never existed so strongly, its legend has never been so flamboyant! It has been enhanced by artists, honored by filmmakers, made ultra competitive by engineers. And racing drivers, now earthly astronauts, push the limits of physics and their own physical strength, the forces of gravity, reaction time.

Frank Williams
Albert Uderzo
Jean Rondeau
Paul Newman
Michèle Mouton
Horacio Pagani
Nigel Mansell
Nick Mason
Ayrton Senna
Quentin Tarantino
Alain Prost
Gildo Pastor

Frank Williams
(b. 1942)

Body and Soul

How do you indulge your passion from the stands?
What is it that drives the F1 managers? Frank Williams
bears witness to both the ruthlessness of the profession
and its understanding of the drivers. He also carries
the scars of his own involvement.

First he had to drive a racing car. And, like any young man who thinks he is a gifted driver, Frank Williams, aged eighteen in 1960, would probably have sold his mother and father for a racing car. Alas, he had to face cruel reality fairly early on: Frank had more enthusiasm than skill. His friend Piers Courage, for instance, was always much faster than him. For all that, Frank got a feel for the atmosphere at the races; he also saw how alone a driver was and how much he needed someone to look after all the logistical aspects of the sport for him. Both an affable and also hard-dealing businessman, Frank was a natural at this. As for his own taste for sport, he satisfied it by becoming a good marathon runner.

Frank organized a structure around Piers Courage, whose skills were confirmed with every race; in the lower formulas first, then very quickly, perhaps too quickly, they went up into Formula 1. This was not unusual for the British, particularly at the end of the Sixties, when most of the cars (Brabham, McLaren, Lotus, then later Surtees, Tyrrell, Ensign, or March) were made up of crafted chassis, built around the excellent and ever-available Cosworth engines. So now we had these unknown people in the spotlight, on the same starting grids as Matra or Ferrari.

Frank Williams understood very quickly that money was there for the taking, as long as each dollar was ploughed back in at once. In his very small company, there was no "limited liability." He was in debt up to his last shirt. Its capacity to soldier on through hard times became one of the hallmarks of the Williams stable. For a few months, he didn't even have a flat to go to, and camped on the sofas of kindly and scarcely better-off friends, who thought he was rather mad anyway. Luckily his lair was on the ground floor near a telephone box where he could receive his business calls; sometimes when he heard the phone ringing and felt the news might be ominous, he would jump out of the window! So he endured poverty all week long and a student diet, and at weekends he was back on the tracks, rubbing shoulders with the nabobs—and beating them sometimes!

His driver became a sort of alter ego, a friend and associate whom he relieved of all racing's trivial aspects and who became Williams's champion, in the medieval sense; a knight who fought his opponents in tournaments to defend his colors.

But the 1969 season brought tragedy. Piers Courage was killed at Zandvoort, driving the de Tomaso Cosworth raced by Williams. It was a shocking setback, calling everything into question. Was all that worth it?

Frank Williams was a racing driver first then set up a stable to help others race (facing page); this was a classic path for managers, but it could still leave a bitter taste in the mouth sometimes.

Halted on the edge of speed (left); knowing how to counsel and criticize the actions of somebody who risks everything on each bend.

Williams leaps a barrier (facing page). Today this keen athlete is confined to a wheelchair, as if fate had wanted to hit him just where it would hurt most.

Terribly upset, Frank Williams fell back on his vice, work, and carried on doing what he did best: running a team. He built his own car but couldn't afford the pleasure of racing it in his own name: that was the main sponsor's privilege. The whole of the Formula 1 scene recognized Frank's very intelligent, very diplomatic, and extraordinary talent for getting a range of exotic backers interested in this marginal and extravagant activity. First of, all Alejandro de Tomaso, then the Italian toymakers Politoys (that was easy: for a few million, every Italian entrepreneur wanted to have a stool with his name on it in the private F1 stands). Next was Walter Wolf, the Canadian oil king, who was so rich that he bought the whole caboodle and threw Frank out. So, in association with a young engineer, Patrick Head—so much more above board in his ways and ability—Frank started from scratch once again, looking for funds. He struck it lucky: he managed to nail Saudia, the airline company, and with them heaven-sent petro-dollars. It was a crucial moment: the Williams racing stable became rich and one of the top teams, at just the moment when the whole sector went through a breathtaking period of increased wealth. Engineers, a brand-new factory, a wind tunnel: Williams could call the tune. Although his income level increased unexpectedly, Frank didn't change his way of life very much and continued to be involved night and day in his stable.

The drivers' status changed within this set-up. Surrounded by press attachés, legal counsel, coaches, they talked on equal terms with the team about extremely lucrative contracts whose big figures made the headlines. In the joust that recruitment had become, Williams wasn't renowned for being too soft. He was still a hyperactive boss, dealing with all aspects of the job, from race strategy to the never-ending questions of finance. In order to relax, he went on long runs, armed with two telephones.

One beautiful day in 1986, traveling on a minor road in the Var district of France, in the warm atmosphere of pine trees and cicadas, Frank tried to get just a bit too much out of his little rented Ford Fiesta. Skid, ditch, somersault resulted in a serious injury to the neck. Frank Williams, the hyperactive man who had reached F1, the driving force behind the Williams team, was now a quadriplegic.

So his passion became a refuge. With the help of Patrick Head, Frank carried on managing the very rich set-up he'd created. Now confined to a wheelchair, he delegates to others by force all the tasks he always used to deal with himself. He has added twelve more world titles to his tally. The ex-marathon runner, now in his carbon-fiber chair, puts all his mental energy into the strategic aspects of Formula 1, especially recruiting the drivers. The drivers…. He always chooses them from among the most ready and willing to fight, the motivated, physical ones; those who will be tough in combat. Working it all out, that's his problem.

For a long time, Frank Williams's legs were his drivers. Nowadays this man, checked in his stride, projects himself alongside them in his mind; it's with his spirit that he races, at speeds nobody can ever equal.

Albert Uderzo

(b. 1927)

Rome, No; Modena, Yes

Albert Uderzo, the co-creator with his partner, Goscinny, of *Asterix the Gaul*, enjoyed traveling, preferably aboard his beloved Ferraris, made in Modena.

The son of an Italian carpenter, Uderzo was born in Marne, the champagne-producing area of northeast France, and chose to side with the Gauls. A long time before creating *Asterix* in 1959, Albert "the Great" was already recognized for the speed at which he worked, which was exceptional given the resulting quality: he could turn out up to five plates a week. You might say that was normal for a carpenter's son. But Uderzo had an objective: to buy himself a car. His big brother, a mechanic, took him to all the races in the Paris region, sometimes to the Grand Prix at Rheims and Rouen, where he saw Fangio, Nuvolari, Hawthorn, and Behra, among others, racing.

In 1949, at last, he had his Simca 5, and a Fiat license: almost an Italian! It was modest, but in the eleventh arrondissement in Paris, his was the only car in the street. In 1951 he got his hands on a Simca Sport, still secondhand. Much later, the memory still vibrant, he told the magazine *Sport Auto*: "I was very proud of that car, I was beginning to show off! I visited Italy with it. When I arrived in small villages, people stopped me and offered me a cigarette to see the engine."

His work began to sell better, and Uderzo climbed up the range: Alfa Spider 2000 then 2600, E Type Jag, etc. His two worlds were not mutually exclusive, and although it was difficult to include drawings of cars in his cartoon strip set in Roman times, he did his best—have a look at *Asterix and the Normans* and young Goudurix's "sports chariot," made in Mediolanum, i.e. Milan!

Then came the enormous, unexpected, and worldwide *Asterix* boom. What did Uderzo buy? A lovely house, with rounded walls and a thatched roof, where he set up his father's old workbench. And then he bought cars, but Ferraris, which was not quite the same thing. He had first seen them racing in 1947. "It was against the turbocharged Alfa Romeo Alfettas. I can still remember the extraordinary noise they made."

Once an active member of the French Ferrari club, he discovered going round racetracks (and going off them, too) and realized—or rather got out of his system—his oldest phantasm, that of being a racing driver. One day he invited his friend Goscinny to see him going round at Castellet. But when he finished, his favorite scriptwriter hurled at him: "Listen, Albert, if you want to finish with life, get a revolver, it'll make less mess." On the contrary, Albert was so convinced that this exercise contributed to improving his safety on the road that he forced his young daughter to take driving lessons at Montlhéry.

The next step was the racing Ferrari he started buying for himself, in particular a P2/P3, of which he still speaks with sobs in his voice. It's a story of two different versions of himself: the skills of the driver he could have been and the child who dreamed of them.

Jean Rondeau

1946-1985

The Man from Le Mans

It's difficult in Milan not to like Opera, in Bordeaux to know nothing about wine, in Rugby not to care a hoot about rugby. In the same way, when Le Mans organizes an extraordinary speed fair every year, it can't fail to impress its velocity-mad children.

Le Mans has been a car capital ever since ... forever! One of the first successful constructors, who was designing, building, and selling automobile machines in 1873, was a man from Le Mans, Amédée Bollée; it's true his *Obéissante* was a steam engine, but it quite definitely drove along the road, not on rails, and went where it wanted to go. Then Le Mans distinguished itself again by being the place where the very first Grand Prix in history was organized in 1906. And after 1923 came the great annual event, the Le Mans 24 Hours race, the archetypal endurance test, which very quickly became a world event, a prestigious objective for the automobile makers and a challenge for the drivers.

Jean Rondeau was from Le Mans. When he was a child, teenager, and later as a young man, he saw the cars going round, he saw the men testing their courage at Les Hunaudières. He wanted to race, he wanted to build, and he wanted to be involved in the sport.

After following a fairly normal career path as a gifted driver, between the Mini Trophies and borrowed cars, between one day successes and everyday financial difficulties, he passed the decisive ten-year mark, when you either break through or you don't. In 1975, he organized a group of interested investors whose object was to put a car in for the 1976 Le Mans race. He built the car in a few months, two versions under the name of Inaltéra, a wallpaper manufacturer and the main sponsor. Rondeau himself took the wheel and finished fourth. He was now a driver and a constructor. The venture's strong point was the incredible reliability of his cars, which reached the checkered flag every time. The weak point was money. Inaltéra had gone and the cars were now under Rondeau's name, but Jean was none the richer—a bit like an author and actor who is also the theater manager. He got further backing from someone from his town, but he also put a lot of his own money into the business and didn't get much out. Despite this, Jean Rondeau's dream came true: at the wheel of his own car, which he had himself designed (helped by a small team of valiant mercenaries), and which bore his name, he won the 1980 Le Mans. This had never happened before and hasn't happened to date since.

The Rondeau make had yet to be built up into something more permanent, but a fantastic and lasting milestone had been reached. His cars took part in all the races. However, when he began to be recognized as a driver as well, Jean drove a more powerful Porsche 956, in which he finished second at the 1982 Le Mans 24 Hours. And, in a strange breach of his own discipline, it was also in a Porsche, a road car this time, that he had a fatal accident in 1985, snatched off a level crossing by the Le Mans–Paris train.

How many young people from Le Mans like Jean Rondeau have dreamed of racing in those long June nights while the 24 Hours race stretches out? He did and he won.

Paul Newman
1925-2008

Fast Forward

Some people believe that true passions always come at a young age. But Paul Newman fell in love with racing at the age of forty-three. And from then on, he never looked back, racing to the end with a beginner's enthusiasm.

He was an actor—and a fine one at that—who admitted that he was absolutely mad about car racing. What luck! At last a learned person who considered speed and driving as worthy of interest: Paul Newman was caught by the racing bug. It was almost as though the racing profession—so often relegated to the role of elementary and brutal hobby—had received the personal endorsement of the likes of Arthur Penn, Alfred Hitchcock, and Martin Scorsese. And of course the films Newman directed himself, very often with the actress Joanne Woodward, (whom he married in Las Vegas and who was with him for fifty years), were hardly mindless action films—just think of the masterly *The Effect of Gamma Rays on Man-in-the-Moon Marigolds*.

Among the others who defected from the job of actor to that of driver there was James Dean, of course, and, more recently again, Patrick Dempsey. Before them there had been Gary Cooper and Clark Gable, who vied with each other on the roads around Hollywood; both had had a very special Duesenberg built in order to race each other and also to shut up Groucho Marx, who had a Mercedes SSK.

Among all these original characters, Paul Newman and Steve McQueen remained special cases in that they learned how to drive seriously and turned out to be among the best. In 1979 Newman was actually runner up in the Le Mans 24 Hours race, and also won the 1995 Daytona 24 Hours in his category, at the age of sixty-nine. Admittedly his status of "paying driver" placed him a notch below the "real" drivers, whose job it really was to race. All the same, taking on the great bend at Les Hunaudières in the rain at more than 180 mph (300 km/h), driving a car as frightening as a Porsche 935 K3, as they say, "took a bit of doing."

As a good pupil of Lee Strasberg and The Actors' Studio, Paul Newman tried to understand the characters he was playing. It was in the film *Winning* (James Goldstone, 1969) that he played the part of a racing driver, in his natural habitat, if you wish: in the great oval circuits that attract the most impressive crowds in world automobile racing. He understood that driving around a circuit was first a question of guts and then, after that, a matter of thought, analysis, and application. It all attracted him.

After that, Newman could not give up racing, and his escapades driving his cars made the headlines on the sports pages of the *Hollywood Chronicle*. In Mel Brooks's *Silent Movie*, a parody of the milieu, he played himself, with one foot in plaster, peacefully reading his newspaper beside his swimming pool whilst a wrecked single-seater, upended like a totem pole, continued to burn. Newman raced for a long time, and even allowed himself to drive briefly again during the Daytona 24 Hours in 2005, aged eighty!

Paul Newman (facing page) trained at The Actors' Studio. Did he get too caught up in the passion needed to do this job when he shot the film *Winning*?

To pretend must be trying sometimes. Somebody else does the stunt and then everybody hurries to get you out of the car, suitably made up. Newman wanted to do everything himself.

But it was in particular as the owner of a stable that he pursued his relationship with the sport. His drivers—especially Sébastien Bourdais, four-time champion under his colors from 2004 to 2007, in the Champ Car World Series—could bear witness to his commitment.

What was it that made Newman race? He did have other commitments; as an actor, of course, but not only that. Running his famous Newman's Own ready-cooked meals company since 1982 could have taken all his time, but he was happy to pay over all the profits, $260 million in less than thirty years, to his favored causes. And he committed himself to the Scott Newman Center, an institution he founded after the death of his eldest son at the age of twenty-eight from depression and no doubt an overdose. That was perhaps why racing entertained him so much: it was certainly a dangerous activity, but it was always recreational and full of light, definitely belonging to the brighter side of life.

Then there is the
fascination with the
machines. It's difficult
to resist an empty
bucket seat, bolted
to a huge engine.

Michèle Mouton
(b. 1951)

A Force of Nature

Michèle Mouton was one of those drivers who raced
first against themselves, to outdo themselves.
In 1982, after winning the rally in Portugal, where
all the most prominent drivers had assembled,
she was in a position where she could win the world title.

"Women drivers." It's not as if there hasn't been enough discrimination on that particular subject! It was even more widespread in the eighties than it is today; all the prejudices that were so pronounced in industry merged with those that were still rife in the world of sport. The combination was pretty explosive. Can you imagine it? A woman taking part in the rally World Championship, and what was more, on the way to winning it! All the world's misogyny underlies that exclamation. But overturning preconceptions is the way to make attitudes change.

Michèle Mouton started driving in the seventies, a bit fortuitously. She navigated for a male rally driver friend, just to see what it was like. But her father, who knew how "spontaneous" her driving could be, wanted to see her behind the wheel. He suggested she race for a year to see if she was good enough to have any hope of going further. Cut to the quick by this challenge, Michèle threw herself into her hobby in an extremely determined way. Her little Alpine saloon became famous very quickly. A few exploits later she was a much sought-after professional driver.

Although Fiat France used heavy 131 Abarths, reputed to be very "physical" to drive, Mouton chalked up a series of results that surprised the men, meaning that she was fighting on equal terms against her teammates and often outclassing

them. Of course, in the regional rallies, there were coarse jokes all the time. In the paddocks there was more than one clown who claimed he'd seen her "peeing against a tree." On the other hand, right at the top, which she wasn't long in reaching, Mouton said that she didn't come across male chauvinism and that the great drivers behaved towards her in a professional way. But among the journalists there were always those drawing attention to the fact that she was a woman in "a man's sport," which was enough to get on the irascible young woman's nerves, since she took it for granted that, in a mechanical sport, only a mixed classification was of any value. For her the very existence of a women's cup was senseless, if not insulting. She accumulated them (six French women's titles and five European ones), but didn't think much of them, and thought that there was no real reason for having two separate classifications.

When Audi put in for the World Championship and made up its team, they included Michèle Mouton in it. Naturally she was recruited with an eye to making publicity. In any case, there she was at the wheel of the Audi Quattro, the best car of the time. For Mouton, as for any other driver, the foremost opponents were her teammates from Audi. And in her first season she won the San Remo rally, one of the races in the World Championship, in front of Henri Toivonen and all the august assembly of

What does it mean
to be the fastest woman
in the world?
For Michèle Mouton
(facing page), it has
always been a matter
of giving it her very best.

Italian drivers. On arrival, she was asked to pose in the tub holding a glass of champagne in her hand. You can imagine her reply!

In 1982, Walter Röhrl was Mouton's main rival throughout the season. He won at Monte Carlo; she won in Portugal. He repeatedly finished in the top three, but she caught up with him by winning the Acropolis and Brazilian rallies, where the German reduced his losses by coming in second. Victory in the Safari rally was vital for both of them. It was a special, long, and backbreaking rally along the East African laterite tracks.

Mouton set off in the lead and got herself well ahead, but a mechanical hitch cancelled this out. There was one stage left. Mouton attacked. In the middle of the night, a patch of fog surprised her and there was an accident. The Quattro did a few high-speed somersaults but luckily Mouton and her copilot, Fabrizia Pons, both came out of it unhurt, so they set off again. But the front running gear had been knocked out of true in the accident, and this put paid to their race for the title when they went off the track again. Tragically, Mouton's father had died a few days before the race, so perhaps—in the great scheme of things—it just wasn't that important any more.

Not in the slightest bit disheartened, Michèle finished runner-up in the last rally, the Lombard RAC. She was runner-up overall in the 1982 World Rally Championship, and Audi won the manufacturers' World Championship for the first time, mainly due to the results she'd obtained.

Other great moments followed, like the hill climb race at Pike's Peak in Colorado. It was one of the most famous in the world, and in the States it was a national event. The difficulty with Pike's Peak was its length (12 ½ miles/20 km with 154 bends) and its altitude at the finish: 14,107 feet (4,301 m). At such altitudes, the engines breathe badly; so do the drivers, who have also climbed too quickly. Not to mention the red earth of the road surface.

In 1985, Audi enlisted Michèle Mouton. The match was well balanced. On one side there were the independent professionals (very well organized and equipped) designing a formula car freely; and on the other side, a factory racing department, with much more financial clout but with an officially approved rally car struggling with very severe rules and restrictions

A European car challenging the local stars: this was okay. But a woman claiming she could beat them: this was a bit too much for these eager chauvinistic and macho spectators. Before a trial climb, Mouton made a strategic error when she heated her tires as usual, with a few raucous starts. The organizers penalized her at once and, in the interests of safety, made her present herself at the start pushed by her mechanics. That meant she had cold tires. Some of her rivals appreciated this unexpected handicap, but they didn't know the Flying Frenchwoman very well. Egged on by the teasing, Mouton outdid herself and triumphed at Pike's Peak, despite all its pitfalls, and then put Colorado well behind her.

Nineteen eighty-six turned out to be her last season, a fabulous season with ten manufacturers lining up their monstrous 500 bhp-plus Group Bs. Mouton was at the summit of her art, recording some of the best times in the world. Jean Todt, the boss of Peugeot, decided to get her to race in the German championship, which she won. But in Corsica, Henri Toivonen and his teammate fell into a ravine and were burnt to death. The Group Bs were banned in favor of the Group As, which were much slower; and so Michèle Mouton put an end to her career. After racing horses, racing mules: no thank you!

At the risk of irritating her, it's worth noting that Mouton still holds the unofficial title of "the fastest woman in the world."

Horacio Pagani
(b. 1960)

Stubborn Dreamer

The time has gone when one man alone designed a car.
Today's cars are a collaborative effort,
guided by marketing and orchestrated by accountants,
except in a few rare cases, like that of Pagani. Just as well:
his is the most beautiful car in the world.

The minute and prestigious car company, Pagani Automobili, is little more than ten years old, but its story started a long time ago in Argentina, where he was born in 1960, when he was asked what he, little Horacio, wanted to do when he grew up.

It was a ritual question, which always embarrassed the child; if he had no idea, he would shift from one foot to the other, rather ill at ease; and if ever he did have an idea, he would be almost shouted at for having so much ambition. So Horacio answered the question as honestly as he could: "I'm going build cars in Modena."

Was it predestined? Maybe. Was he very determined? Certainly. In the entrance hall of the company, Modena Design, which he founded some forty years later, a little shelf still displays a few children's models, pure inventions, which bear witness to his unfailing determination. Discreetly and resolutely, he became an engineer and a stylist, got experience building Formula 3 cars, then joined Lamborghini in 1983 as an employee before simply deciding to do better than his bosses.

This lively little man, whose intense blue eyes twinkled behind his glasses, had something childlike, something implacable in his movements, and especially in his enthusiasm. He could speak for hours about his Zonda (from the name of an Argentine wind). In order to obtain a few hours of intimacy with this workaholic, his wife set out to receive the press and organize car shows. There is one detail: every one of the twenty-five people who work for Horacio has been able to drive the car, so it's not surprising that they are united by the same team spirit. And the boss is there. He works a lot, dividing his time between the design office and the building of his Zondas, whose every step he follows with shining eyes.

For the next installment, it's the car that takes up the tale. The stunning silhouette was inspired by the Group C endurance cars. Each mechanical part is exactly what it has to be, conceived with the same specifications and at the same expense as those for a racing car. For example, Pagani x-rays the aluminum on each suspension triangle to make sure that it has been correctly molded. For the bodywork and the shell, everything is made of carbon. When you open the bonnet you won't find a single component less smooth, less varnished, or less well finished than another. In the smallest of corners, behind the seats, under the steering wheel, the carbon's brilliance awaits the curious visitor, worked with such care that its blackness has become light, and all things technical the most beautiful of ornaments.

A factory made of glass, and cars made of carbon: a dream come true for Horacio Pagani (facing page), the eternal admirer of shapes, techniques, and speed.

Carbon was chosen because it is light and rigid, but Pagani surrounds this high-tech substance with a veritable liturgy, going so far as to offer—bearing in mind the 500,000 euros each car already costs—an unpainted car in bare carbon, each fiber being smoothened and arranged with the greatest care.

In accordance with his oldest dreams, Pagani installed his factory near Modena, like Ferrari, Maserati, de Tomaso, Lamborghini, and so many others had done. In the little glass building, you won't find those long corridors so clearly separating the drudges from the deciders, isolating the latter from the noises of the workshops. Here, push open a door and you discover the manufacturing hall, without mystery but not without magic. Entering gives you an almost religious sensation.

Within this space, they are busy readying the fastest road cars of all: 212 mph (340 km/h) for the latest 7.3-liter Zonda S. In these days of speed restrictions, this center of worship looks more like an opium smoker's underground den, a resistance fighter's lair, even a temple.

A road car which goes as fast as that is actually of no use, but it's a superb machine, a sublime prosthesis which compensates for the weak physical capacities of two-legged creatures, and enables them to inhabit the countryside as they move into it, to move around in space at the speed of their imagination, to get close to being ubiquitous; a state that should be ours by right but which has been denied us by Nature. That's quite something.

During the bold years of our childhood, many of us have dreamed of creating a car, our own car, imagining its structural design, drawing its outlines. But very few have actually been able to take the idea further, and instead we all drive around in our mass-produced cars. Horacio Pagani dreamed of tailor-made cars; today he has his place in automobile's *haute couture*. You see: it was possible.

Of all the expensive cars we might dream about, the Paganis are the finest hand-finished models.

If Pagani was a sculptor,
we would be spellbound
by his art. And even more
magical: some
of these models even drive
themselves.

Nigel Mansell
(b. 1953)

The Many Adventures of Nigel

Nigel Mansell, 1992 World Champion, really was one of the best drivers in the world. But as well as having an exceptional top speed, this big chap was rather prone to making gaffes, making him all the more unforgettable.

After the Grand Prix there was a press conference. Nelson Piquet entertained his audience of newspapermen (together with 600 million viewers) with an account of his race, punctuated with witty, snide remarks about his rivals. Alain Prost interested his audience by giving extraordinarily fine analyses to explain his choice of tuning to match the circuit's features. Ayrton Senna impressed his audience by taking apart the tenth of a second he put between himself and his rivals. When Nigel Mansell took over the mike, he said: "Thanks to all the team and the mechanics who did a fantastic job." Very nice, except that this was almost word for word what he was to say each time he had a good race, during his fifteen seasons in F1. Good old Nigel.

It was at Estoril in Portugal on September 24, 1989 that, leading with his Ferrari, Mansell returned to the pits to change his Goodyear tires. In too much of a hurry, he overshot his stand by a good five yards; still in too much of a hurry, he reversed to reposition himself, which was forbidden and had been so for ages. He set off again, was given the disqualifying black flag for his mistake but, still in too much of a hurry, he didn't see it for a whole lap, didn't see it for two laps, even three laps. It has to be said that he caught up with Senna, though of course that would not count. Still in too much of a hurry, he overtook him, and continuing to press

hard, got his Ferrari caught with the Brazilian's McLaren at 188 mph (300 km/h). He lost his license for one race and was fined $50,000 dollars. His morale took a blow.

In Mexico on June 24, 1990, with one lap to go, Mansell, delayed by another car going into a spin, was third behind Prost's Ferrari and Berger's McLaren. Berger was a fast driver and difficult to overtake. Bend after bend, with the finish getting close, the two single-seaters came into the Peraltada, a long, deep bend, sloping slightly and very fast. Mansell had got a few mph more by following in the McLaren's slipstream. With all the daring that he was known for, he changed lanes, just at the entrance to this impressive bend, at the moment when any reasonable-minded driver would have lifted his foot off the accelerator slightly, and overtook the McLaren on the outside, instinctively inaugurating a new way round that bend which turned out to be practicable, just like when a mountaineer hammers pitons for the first time into the north face of some long-forbidden summit, other mountaineers watch the exploit and say, "Ah, so it was possible, after all."

Suzuka, Japan, on October 21, 1990. Mansell was in the lead and stopped at his stand. Not wanting to stall, he kept his Ferrari's V-12 engine revs high, but when the single-seater was lowered back to the ground, he declutched so

Among the drivers, there are the perfectionists, the tacticians, and the strategists. And then there was Mansell (facing page), who was none of those, but who at one time was the purest talent in Formula 1.

sharply that the transmission literally exploded. The Ferrari covered a few yards pitifully under its own momentum. Mansell lifted his arms to heaven.

Montreal on June 2, 1991. The Williams-Renault had won the race and was coasting along more than a minute ahead of the runner-up, Nelson Piquet. Nigel Mansell was as happy as a sand boy, his arms outside the cockpit, waving to his team, the public, and the course officials. The Williams was gradually slowing down and this last parade lap was unending; the engine was going so slowly that the V-10 Renault started snorting and gasping and ended up stalling, and with the engine went all the systems that control the gearbox and the brakes. Mansell could not put the engine into gear, nor start the engine again. Five opponents sailed past him. He had won so well that he found the way of actually losing!

Magny-Cours on July 5, 1991. In an invincible, frenzied whirl, Mansell had overtaken Senna, Patrese, and finally Prost one after the other, overtaking with a magnificent "outsider" on the Adelaide hairpin. He was on the top step of the podium and there, overcome by emotion, he cried during his National Anthem. Standing to attention in front of him, listening to the anthem that was paying tribute to the Englishman, was François Mitterrand, master political manipulator, satisfied with the public acclaim for this new circuit, which his ministers had wanted; there was also Jean-Marie Balestre, Formula 1's bogeyman and formidable president of the Federation. Beside Mansell were Ayrton Senna and Alain Prost who were sworn enemies. What did Mansell do, all overcome with tears as he was? He grabbed his rivals in his great big paws and drew them towards him on the top step. Nigel Mansell was so happy that he wanted everybody to love each other!

Silverstone in England on July 12, 1992: Mansell was in the lead in the World Championship with six victories and just couldn't stop winning, and this was despite the speed of his teammate Ricardo Patrese, who admitted to being outdriven, despite Senna's McLaren-Honda and Schumacher's Benetton-Ford, despite also his own country's press, which rambled on about Mansell's blunders and tried to convince its readers of their "champion's" limited intellectual capacities. It was because of these not always very chivalrous remarks against him that, when the flag was finally lowered, the supposedly aloof crowd of his supporters invaded the track, forcing all the other cars to stop. Mansell was removed from his seat, half smothered by the crowd, and carried away

in triumph. An ambulance was needed to force a way through the crowd, kidnap him and take him to the podium! Fantastic! Surfers Paradise, Australia in 1993: F1 World Championship title holder, Mansell, not finding a race which was paid enough for his liking, left the top discipline of the European circuits for the CART Indy Car World Series championship, the top event for American-style single-seaters. This was new terrain, new car, new circuit; everything had to be learnt again. The first race took place in Australia; this was his first try. Was it a success? Well, yes: he got pole position and won. He went on to win the 1993 CART championship before the F1 1993 championship had been decided, becoming the first person ever to hold the F1 championship and CART championship titles at the same time. Quite an adventure.

No more mustaches? Was this to lighten the car? Mansell is still racing (left). Here he is in the Masters Grand Prix, a competition for old champions, which he won against Patrese (on the right) and Fittipaldi.

Nick Mason
(b. 1944)

A Sound Investment

The destinies of celebrities often take unexpected turns.
Nick Mason, Pink Floyd's drummer, could have sat
on his laurels and simply lapped up the success earned back
in the days as a rock star. Instead he took to collecting racing cars
and that has now become much more than just a hobby.

He is a musician in one of the most famous groups of all time, and a good amateur driver. The double miracle is that Mason has remained modest! His group's extraordinary successes have freed him from the dreaded "hit," and he continues to make the music he likes making, within the old group or with Carla Bley on the album *Fictitious Sports*. The fact that he could afford almost any car freed him from the need to find ever-increasing power, and he collected his cars according to the sensations they produced in him. In his book (*Into the Red*, Virgin Books, 1998) he gives us an enjoyable, unique account, in which he compares his cars from the point of view of the amateur collector/ driver. It consists of twenty-two car portraits and, at the same time, implicitly, is a self-portrait, coupled with a definition of pleasure and a few confessions about the difficult situation of the rich buyer.

Among Mason's favorite cars, first up is the 1960 Maserati Birdcage (2.9 liters, 240 bhp, 147 mph, 1,320 lb). Of its reincarnation in 2005 he has said: "I've driven a number of real concept cars, and this was streets ahead. I've driven some that look fabulous but drive like tea-trolleys, whereas the Birdcage 75th was a complete car. And it's the most wonderful looking car of all."

Among the fundamental elements of his personal taste—and may this list awaken the profane among you to the pleasure, the true pleasure, you can still find when you drive a quality machine—you can note the style of the interior with his preference for a classic interior, i.e., round instruments and wooden steering wheel. Next there is a certain ease of driving. Regarding his 1970 Ferrari 512 S (V-12, 5000 cc, 550 bhp, 196 mph, 1, 848 lb), Mason claims he must have been suffering from a dangerous bout of over-confidence when he bought it. If he had thought twice, he might have realized that the only drivers who had been successful at the wheel of this machine were among the best of all time (and some of them were no longer around).

Finally for Nick Mason, among the criteria which go to make a great car, there is obviously music.

World champion from 1962 to 1964, twice runner-up at Le Mans (from scratch), the Ferrari 250 GTO (V-12, 3000 cc, 300 bhp, 171 mph, 2, 299 lb) is one of the most expensive collector's cars: it costs around twenty million dollars. Nick was lucky to be able to afford his when he bought it back in the seventies, before the prices reached unreasonable heights. It would be logical for him

Nick Mason (facing page) collects spicy driving impressions, just as Pink Floyd went about chasing after unheard-of sounds.

to stash it away in a bank vault. And yet, following another logic, he sometimes races it, and come what may.

As for what it is that triggers his enthusiasm, there is the old argument that dreams can come true. Among the thirty-five Ferrari GTOs ever built, Mason noticed after he had bought it that he had acquired the very same one he had photographed as a young man as it went through the chicane at Goodwood.

Some destinies deserve a drum roll.

For a musician from Pink Floyd, admitting to loving cars in the Sixties might have caused his fans some upset. This said, posing next to a photogenic model was in keeping with Masson's image. Here he is at the back leaning on the trunk.

To drive a rare car, the best thing to do is to buy it. But sometimes there are opportunities, like this invitation from the Audi Museum to try out a 1930s Auto Union.

Ayrton Senna
1960-1994

"Magic" Senna

His death saddened more than just Formula 1 racing fans. It roused millions of people throughout the world from their indifference. His spectacular driving, his position as an idol in Brazil, and his incredible—and merciless—battles with Alain Prost were so impressive, he had come to represent the ultimate racing driver. He was fast, he was a winner, there was something magical about him, and—as people suddenly remembered—he was ever so fragile.

Happy he who for Fame or Liberty
In strength's full pride
and dream's enrapturing bliss,
Dies such undaunted, dazzling death as this[1]

This ends the poem by José Maria de Héredia, "Death of an Eagle," which describes an eagle that has flown too high. There was something of this in Senna, though he lacked neither strength nor pride. Apart from the other characteristics common to all high-level racing drivers—aggressiveness, authority, an ability to cheat when necessary, etc.—Senna possessed something else, something purer: a liking for going beyond things, of obtaining the absolute performance, almost of art for art's sake. Any sportsman, any craftsman committed to doing something perfectly comes very near to this sort of sublime moment. Senna seemed to have made it into a personal ideal.

His very brutal death caused an enormous storm in the media. F1 fans embarked on a technical analysis of the accident that would continue for years; more than fifteen years after that fateful Imola Grand Prix, they're still at it. Some preferred to put forward the idea that there was some mechanical failure (the steering had indeed broken), which meant the aura of an inspired driver remained intact. At any rate, the black box in his Williams-Renault was quite unable to determine what it was that caused him to leave the track, but it did give a faithful rendering of the extraordinary way he braked on the grass in front of the rail, during that second in which he managed to reduce his speed by more than 60 mph (100 km/h), so that when the Williams-Renault hit the rail it was going at "only" 131 mph (210 km/h), but it was still far too much.

Others preferred by far to think that, if he went off the track, it was "driver's error," that he himself made a mistake, perhaps because he had been too close to the inside lane bumps he had warned his teammate, Damon Hill, about during the trials; perhaps because he had misjudged the road-holding of the tires—they would have cooled down after several laps behind the security car; or perhaps because for a tenth of a second he had lost that exact balance between aggressiveness and safety, that sensitivity to movement which makes all the

There were great mystics, great warriors, and great poets, all with that look (facing page).

Senna's driving ranged from Prost-like clarity to quite extraordinary agility, including in Formula 1. Here, he is in a McLaren, in 1988.

difference between victory and catastrophe, that almost incredible accuracy which was all his art. A mistake doesn't cast any doubt upon a driver's capabilities; it stresses the difficulties he is facing.

Racing in general, and Formula 1 in particular, is a paradoxical art. A car going round a circuit, even very fast, just makes the spectator feel drowsy; it's just a routine exploit. As long as there's no fight between two drivers, mudguard to mudguard, the layman gets bored, the fan is disappointed. Sometimes the driver himself just does his job, is content to excel. But the moment the car leaves its expected path, it becomes a terrifying machine. The sterile, advertising-overloaded background created for television's two-dimensional world, becomes once again a nightmarish succession of obstacles: the vibrator, the rail, and the fencing all suddenly take on their full weight of inert matter against which the 600 kg (two-thirds of a ton) of an F1 car can only crash, its momentum crushed.

Now we don't go to the racetracks to see drivers getting themselves killed. We go to see them escaping death, taming danger—though they do get as close as possible to it. To transcend the fatality of matter, they no doubt have to have that pressure in their guts, that energy which moves from the guts to the spirit.

Senna was a driving virtuoso, just like any other sort of artistic virtuoso. Above all, he had to be the best and get to the summit of his art, subordinating his whole life to that purpose. Of course, Senna was no yogi. But, by his own admission, this fervent Catholic kept up an unceasing dialogue with the

Eternal. Each time he got into his car, prayer was a way of perfecting his concentration.

At the age of four, he was given a go-kart and took part in his first races when he was fourteen. From that moment onwards, a whole lifetime's work started: winning and improving all the time. He was big enough, but he did have a rather frail constitution. With help from a personal coach who did not spare him, he forged himself an athlete's body: fine, solid muscles, good breathing and the heart rate of an Olympian. Was he worse when the ground was wet? Having once lost a go-kart race because of a shower, he transformed this liability into a strength. He started watching the sky and took advantage of the rare rainy days in São Paulo, getting his car out every time to improve his mastery. He became a legendary rain-master, almost invincible on rainy surfaces.

There followed a meteoric rise, common to all gifted drivers. He agreed to leave his dear Brazil and exile himself for four years in the mists of England, a country where the competition in the "junior" formulas was keener and therefore more testing. Although he came from a well-off family, he didn't have enough money to live in luxury. And his passion was so all-devouring that his marriage to Lillian, his childhood sweetheart, was sorely put to the test. There was a moment when, discouraged by financial difficulties, Senna gave up racing, but after several months during which Lillian looked after their flat while he worked for his father's big agency, his desire to race became too strong and he returned to England. Lillian let him go alone. *De facto* separated, they divorced several months later.

Formula Ford 1600 in 1981: 12 victories and the title. Formula Ford 2000 in 1982: 21 out of 27 possible wins. Formula 3 in 1982: 12 victories out of 20 races and the title; he left the track several times, each time fighting it out with Martin Brundle. At aged twenty-four, Ayrton reached Formula 1.

Alain Prost became the young man's target. Beating him would mean he'd reached the top. From his first season onwards, and despite a rather ordinary car (Toleman-Hart), in which he only qualified at the rear of the grid, he almost won the Monaco Grand Prix—in the rain, of course, which was so heavy that the race had to be interrupted, right under the nose of the Toleman, which was about to swallow Prost's McLaren whole! How frustrating. But Senna's skill had been spotted, and he was now one of the small number of drivers that the stables fought over. It was Lotus that got hold of him, but the team was in difficulty: only six victories in three seasons.

Senna fine-tuned his talent. His engineers, especially Gérard Ducarouge, were astounded by the precision of the technical details he gave them. The Honda engine builders swore only by him. His boundless technical commitment during the private trials, his quest for the ideal lap during the qualifications (he gained 68 pole positions), his physical commitment during the races; all this united the people around him and electrified the public. There was always something left for him to conquer. Almost unbeatable in the art of obtaining the fastest lap time, Senna seemed to be searching a personal accomplishment through pure speed, by getting the best time.

All F1 was waiting for "the day when Senna would be driving a good car." He got it in 1988 with McLaren, alongside Alain Prost. Already crowned twice with this team, Prost was not averse to the challenge of putting the arrogant Brazilian back in his place. But Senna got ahead and his record took off. The struggle between the two men became a bitter psychological struggle. Behind the scenes there were a lot of punches below the belt, and in public the "racing incidents" multiplied. On two occasions the title was fought out between them during the Japanese Grand Prix. In 1988, a contentious bump turned to Prost's advantage and he pocketed the title since he had more points. In 1990, Senna was championship leader, and the fact that the two cars had to abandon the race did not affect him. He deliberately provoked an incident in which the cars left the track at high

speed, but he only owned up to it a year later, which was an almost unique, unpardonable act, especially at that speed, especially as the Grand Prix had been televised live worldwide.

Nevertheless, Senna was now an idol. But it took him two further seasons before he could get his hands on the best car of the time. In 1994 he joined Frank Williams's team in place of Prost, who at the time held the World Championship with that particular car. Prost withdrew, refusing to team up with Senna again.

Senna was now the logical favorite, the reigning idol, whom the others wanted to beat. The first two races suggested there would be a struggle with a certain Michael Schumacher. But all that would change on the great bend at Imola on May 1, 1994.

1. Translation by Edward Robeson Taylor.

Quentin Tarantino
(b. 1963)

The Artful Dodge

Tarantino likes anything that smacks of heresy.
He's the cinematic equivalent of a bookworm, whose taste
veers from intellectual arthouse films to the scariest B movies.

Ever heard of Knoxville? It's at the junction of two interstates, Route 40 leading east toward Nashville (184 miles) and west toward Kingsport (86 miles), and Route 75 northwards to Cincinnati (220 miles). It's a little American town with four hundred churches, twenty cinemas, and countless garages, in a slow and quiet little province caught up in modernity's not-so-exciting routine.

Tarantino is today the good town of Knoxville's most famous child. Having said this, as a teenager it must have been far too sleepy for his liking and you can just imagine how he must have dreamed of getting away. Anything that enabled him to do that would have been all the more appealing: movies provided a form of escapism and, of course, so did cars.

In his films, Quentin Tarantino endlessly recycles the origins of his teenage imagination: B movies, screenplays imitating pulp fiction and of course, muscle cars: those over-vamped cheap coupés with which American manufacturers flooded the market in the 1960s and 1970s, following on the huge success of the Ford Mustang, cars like the Chevrolet Camaro, Dodge Charger, Buick Regal and Plymouth Barracuda.

In many a film, Tarantino taps into the gorier aspects of car imagery and is not afraid to exploit its major fetishes, particularly in *Death Proof* (2007). On a more playful note, he clearly loves great stunts. The most obvious example of this might be the Dodge Challenger RT car chase in *Death Proof*, in which a stuntwoman rolls around on the hood of a moving car. The scene is a clear homage to the action-road movie *Vanishing Point* (Richard Sarafian, 1971).

The audience also takes guilty pleasure from watching that kind of scene. Continuing the example of *Death Proof*, if at the last moment the woman driver turned the wheel sharply and avoided the collision, viewers would be disappointed. Tarantino explains this for us: "That's the thing: to get them complicit, get them wanting it and waiting for it. Then—BANG!—it happens, it's so much more horrible than you ever could have imagined. But … too late! You wanted it to happen. You willed it into being. You are complicit in it. Now take your medicine!"

Tarantino drives his films a long way to the edge of the precipice with an assumed complaisance for sordidness, cocking a snook in the direction of the demons he awakens. Skeptical, passionate, amused, and horrified, we follow him in the many twists and turns and abrupt changes in gear that make up his films, marveling at his virtuosity when he directs actors And what actors! Chevrolet Nova SS, Ford Mustang Fastback, Dodge Charger R/T. Spot a scary reoccurring pattern? Needless to say, the collector value of muscle cars has tripled since Tarantino's film came out!

Playing with excitement and fear, playing with finer feelings and morbid urges, and therefore playing with cars, obviously (facing page).

Alain Prost
(b. 1955)

Anatomy of a Champion

Whoever tries to turn his passion into a reality, and to make a career of it, may also lose sight of it. Alain Prost, the archetype of the analytical racing driver, may have appalled lovers of fiery driving by his critical aloofness, but beneath the love of winning lay the love of driving.

A passion is not just a hobby to which you apply talent. Passion is something that we are unable to tear from ourselves; it's something that shapes us. Alain Prost never imagined he would ever be far from car racing. However, the epithet "passionate" is not the first thing that springs to mind when you mention the four-time World Champion; he's such an archetypal professional! It's like asking Lance Armstrong whether he likes cycling!

Alain Prost also liked football. But he was small, slender and, on a football pitch, as the big guys explained very quickly, a sense of where to send the ball and how to use your feet were just not enough to score all the goals, and a twisted nose and a broken knee soon kept him away from that particular terrain.

Fortunately Prost discovered go-karts. In this sport, being small is vital. And he won his first race. He saved up, penny by penny, to buy a chassis and a suit. Prost later recalled that this was actually the only money this allegedly elitist sport ever cost him. Yes, but then he can't really be regarded as typical because he *is* extremely capable. Prost then followed a path you could consider as "normal": first go-karting from sixteen onwards, winning the French and European titles, then the Volant Elf. This trophy rewards a driving school, and at the time was a real door-opener:

winning it meant a season with Renault with a car provided and serviced. On the morning of the semi final of this famous Volant, he arrived late. The other competitors did a couple of laps, one after the other, driving the school's single-seaters. Prost later admitted that he'd arrived late deliberately: he wanted to see how each car performed and choose the best for his own laps.

Signing up with Formula Renault, he was champion, winning twelve out of thirteen races. In 1977 he pocketed the Formula Renault European title, but less easily. In 1979, he won two F3 titles. During this rise, Prost constantly surprised people with his maturity and his analytical abilities. The team manager and talent spotter, Hugues de Chaunac, became totally fascinated by his protégé. For instance, to see how sharp the young drivers' technical analysis was, this mentor liked to change the angle of the aileron by just one degree on the quiet. If the driver didn't feel anything, he would add a degree, and so on. The first time he tested Prost like that, Prost immediately stopped in the pits and asked him why he had touched his aileron.

Alain Prost very quickly earned the nickname "Professor." A rather paradoxical tendency now accompanied his rise. In the paddocks, among the drivers, he was thought of as a role model, but he

Few angry outbursts, little enthusiasm, but lots of sulking and infinite application. Prost (facing page), who was an extraordinarily fast driver, was a man with slow-burning moods.

had few, if any, friends. Was he too brilliant? No doubt, but he was also too much of an analyst, too taken up with the importance of a job that never lets up. Once again, de Chaunac remembers how exacting and intransigent the young Prost could be. After winning, most drivers relaxed; many lived it up. Not Prost: after five minutes' joy, he'd start counting his points in the championship, talking strategy again, and plunging the team into long technical debriefings to check, comment, and try to get to the bottom of all the problems that had cropped up.

Prost managed his career by himself. He decided to turn down Formula 2 races and go straight into Formula 1 with McLaren. He did a try-out with them, along with another young driver, Kevin Cogan. Not only did Prost dishearten Cogan by relegating him to three seconds, but on top of that he clocked up better times than the team's driver, John Watson, who'd been in F1 for seven years. And although newcomers to F1 are usually a bit awed by the standard of the performances, Prost's reaction was quite different: "As for the power, it's marvelous because in F3 you always want to go faster. But even then, now even though it's thrusting terribly as you come out of the bends, as soon as you get the hang of things, you want it to give even more power. At any rate the more you've got, the more you want...."[1]

The best motivation imaginable is getting amazing results immediately: he even scored points in his first two Grand Prix. His subsequent career looked much more like a reign.

When he reluctantly gave up F1, Alain Prost wound up the discipline's best tally of prizes, all periods included (since then, only Michael Schumacher has outdone him): 51 victories, 33 pole positions, 41 best lap times during a race, 4 times champion, 4 times runner-up, 798.5 points; a score which he obtained in thirteen seasons, during which he also learnt how to adapt to all the different technical changes the profession was going through, including 1,500 horsepower-plus turbocharged engines during qualifications, at the beginning of the eighties.

Less capped drivers were more adept at earning the spectators' affection, though. There were two reasons for this. Firstly, Alain's driving

was a miracle of mechanical precision and balance, but seen from the trackside it certainly lacked warmth. Secondly, he was almost as skillful a politician as he was a clever driver, so when he raced he was always driving the best car. During the Prost era, Formula 1's dramatic intensity moved from the track to behind the scenes. The enthusiastic spectator had to forget phrases like "controlled spin" and learn instead "team motivation," "discussions with the engineers," "psychological pressure." His duels with Niki Lauda (whom he dominated on the circuits, but who did manage to "control" him for a whole year), then later with Senna (who was faster than him, but whom Prost often destabilized) took on another, more astounding guise when they were in this register. Naturally, these great changes were not his doing. Huge tires, ground effect, and then electronic assistance have favored the technical drivers, to the detriment of the more extrovert talents. The car's pre-eminence over the drivers, which had never been so clearly established, was what favored the strategists.

Alain Prost gave the racing driver's role all its intellectual and political breadth, so much so that we may have forgotten that it is passion, the only true driving force, which keeps our foot down when we turn into a blind bend at almost 190 mph (300 km/h).

Later, Prost founded his own F1 stable; it was at first an exalting then a painful episode, overall more of a business than a passion. Even later he took part in the Andros Trophy, a series of races on ice between seasons. It's a discipline in which you have to drive and slide all over the place, whereas Prost has always advocated driving straight. What on earth was the four-time World Champion doing there? The fifty-year-old who has got nothing left to prove behind the steering wheel? The billionaire who's living in Switzerland? Maybe he's just carrying on with his passion?

1. Interview with *Auto-Hebdo*, 1979. (Our translation)

So rarely jingoistic, Prost nonetheless grabbed the French flag to celebrate his fourth World Championship, in the Portuguese Grand Prix (left). Was this just to humiliate a certain Brazilian?

The Formula 1 driver, a modern centaur, in his single-seater, which is almost molded round him. He's master on board (below).

Gildo Pallanca Pastor

(b. 1967)

Highly Charged

Gildo Pastor knew everything about cars. As a Monegasque millionaire, being exceptional was his everyday fare. That's why perhaps, having bought the Venturi Company, he gave it such a categorically different assignment from the others: to reconcile electric cars and the concept of enjoyment.

Little Gildo saw stunning cars, hordes of them, in his father's garage, filling the casino garage, and parked all around Monaco, his home town. It is a town that even dares to ban all automobiles from its narrow avenues for one week a year just for the F1 craze. Super!

This privileged kid was often to be seen waiting, sitting at the wheel of a single-seater, in the Place Beltoise or Place Stewart. All this was quite contagious. To make matters worse, the whole family was mad about cars, even the grandfather, the last link with a not-so-wealthy past, who had never given up repairing trucks.

For some, juvenile delinquency is stealing bicycles. With the Pastors, it was more spectacular: at the age of twelve, little Gildo started borrowing the family's cars, which very often weren't 2CVs. Of course, he naturally drove very fast, to the great despair of his family, until youth spent itself.

When he finally pocketed his driving license, Gildo did not slow down. On the contrary, he rushed to take part in races. Rallies, circuits, in Europe, or the United States, on tarmac, earth, or ice—a whole collection of sensations, with a few victories: particularly the Chamonix 24 Hours, and a speed record on ice in a Bugatti EB 110: 185.21 mph (296.34 km/h). Gildo always knew the exact figure by heart to the last decimal place.

When Gildo broke with cars, he didn't actually give them up. He ran a racing team and then took over Venturi, a recent French name in sports cars, which was a courageous venture though always in the red. Gildo had his own idea: an electric sports car. The idea bowled everybody over, including his own little outfit, which was run by a Formula 1 engineer, Gérard Ducarouge.

This far-fetched idea was turned into an unprecedented car which, for the first time in the context of automobile engineering, used the features of electricity to generate pleasure. The light little craft accelerated like a Ferrari but in total silence, at least where the engine was concerned. Both driver and passenger could hear the sound of big tires as they never had before; the torque was constant from standstill; engine breaking was adjustable on the dashboard and spared the wheel brakes; you were still driving a sports car but it felt different. The sensualist had invented a new delight and an alternative to "petro-hedonism"!

Pastor at the wheel of his Venturi Astrolab (facing page): nanotechnological solar panels, sophisticated batteries, zero gas emissions, a range of 75 miles, and a full tank of enthusiasm!

Index

Picture Credits